The Nineteenth Amendment

Other titles in *The Constitution* series:

The First Amendment
Freedom of Speech, Religion, and the Press
ISBN: 0-89490-897-9

The Second Amendment
The Right to Own Guns
ISBN:0-89490-925-8

The Fourth Amendment
Search and Seizure
ISBN: 0-89490-924-X

The Fifth Amendment
The Right to Remain Silent
ISBN: 0-89490-894-4

The Thirteenth Amendment
Ending Slavery
ISBN: 0-89490-923-1

The Fifteenth Amendment
African-American Men's Right to Vote
ISBN: 0-7660-1033-3

The Eighteenth and Twenty-First Amendments
Alcohol—Prohibition and Repeal
ISBN: 0-89490-926-6

The Nineteenth Amendment
Women's Right to Vote
ISBN: 0-89490-922-3

The Nineteenth Amendment

Women's Right to Vote

The
Constitution

Judy Monroe

Enslow Publishers, Inc.

40 Industrial Road	PO Box 38
Box 398	Aldershot
Berkeley Heights, NJ 07922	Hants GU12 6BP
USA	UK

http://www.enslow.com

Library of Congress Cataloging-in-Publication Data

Monroe, Judy
    The Nineteenth Amendment : women's right to vote / Judy Monroe.
      p. cm. — (The Constitution)
    Includes bibliographical references and index.
    Summary: Traces the history of the women's rights movement in the
United States which culminated in 1920 with the passage of the
constitutional amendment giving women the right to vote.
    ISBN 0-89490-922-3
    1. Women—Suffrage—United States—History—Juvenile literature.
2. United States. Constitution. 19th Amendment—History—Juvenile
literature. 3. Constitutional amendments—United States. [1. Women—
Suffrage—History. 2. United States. Constitution. 19th Amendment—
History. 3. Constitutional amendments.] I. Title.
II. Series: Constitution (Springfield, Union County, N.J.)
KF4895.Z9M6   1998
324.6'2'0973—DC21   97-23363
                                            CIP
                                            AC

10 9 8 7 6 5

Photo Credits: Gene Garrett, Minnesota Historical Society, p. 57;
League of Women Voters Archives, p. 84; Library of Congress, pp. 23,
39, 47, 52, 54, 68; National Archives, pp. 8, 11, 30, 65, 89; Richard Bartl,
p. 91.

Cover Photo: AP/Wide World Photos

Contents

The Birth of Women's Suffrage

For two summer days in 1848, over three hundred men and women sat or stood in the Wesleyan Methodist Chapel, a small church in Seneca Falls, New York. The audience listened for hours to speeches about women's rights—and lack of rights. After many discussions, the Seneca Falls group passed a Declaration of Sentiments on Friday, July 20, 1848.

The declaration contained a number of resolutions, or specific requests. Resolution Nine stated that women should have the right to vote. This marked the birth of the women's suffrage movement. This movement eventually resulted in the the Nineteenth Amendment to the United States Constitution, which was passed on August 26, 1920. The amendment guarantees American women the right to vote.

The Seneca Falls meeting was the first time a large group of people met to establish a set of equal rights principles for women, including the vote. Their goal was to make the principles become law.

Elizabeth Cady Stanton was one of the organizers of the Women's Rights Convention at Seneca Falls, New York, in 1848. She was also the first president of the National Woman Suffrage Association.

Credit for this history-making event goes to the five women organizers: Jane Hunt, Mary Ann McClintock, Lucretia Mott, Elizabeth Cady Stanton, and Martha C. Wright.

Launching a Daring Plan

Friends Elizabeth Cady Stanton and Lucretia Mott first met at an antislavery convention, a group of meetings in London, England, in 1840. Since then, they had continued to discuss equal rights for women. By 1848, Stanton was ready for more. "I could not see what to do or where to begin—my only thought was a public meeting for protest and discussion."[1]

To further develop her idea, Stanton visited her friend Lucretia Mott in Waterloo, New York, near Seneca Falls, on July 13, 1848. When she arrived at the Mott home, she found three other friends there: Jane Hunt, Mary Ann McClintock, and Martha C. Wright. The five women sat around a table. While Elizabeth Cady Stanton spoke the others all listened. In her autobiography, Stanton recalled, "I poured out, that day, the torrent of my long-accumulating discontent, with such vehemence and indignation that I stirred myself, as well as the rest of the party, to do and dare anything."[2]

Her outpouring, Stanton recalled, "moved us all to prompt action, and we decided, then and there, to call a 'Women's Rights Convention.'"[3] To announce the convention, the group wrote a notice. It was published the next day in the local newspaper, the *Seneca County Courier*:

> Women's Rights Convention—A convention to discuss the social, civil, and religious rights of women will be held in the Wesleyan Chapel, Seneca Falls, New York, on Wednesday and Thursday, the 19th and 20th of July current; commencing at 10 A.M. During the first day the

meeting will be held exclusively for women, who are earnestly invited to attend. The public generally are invited to be present on the second day, when Lucretia Mott of Philadelphia and other ladies and gentlemen will address the convention.[4]

The women next decided to write a Declaration of Sentiments. They struggled with how to put together their declaration. Elizabeth Cady Stanton suggested using the Declaration of Independence as a model. When the others agreed, Stanton, following the Declaration of Independence, wrote, "We hold these truths to be self-evident that all men and women are created equal."[5]

The five women together wrote an introduction and a list of women's grievances. Stanton was then given the job of writing the resolutions of women. She developed twelve resolutions. The wording of the actual resolutions is complicated and somewhat difficult to understand, but each resolution dealt with an individual right that all women should have.

Stanton did not tell her four friends about Resolution Nine, which demanded the vote for women. Perhaps she was concerned, based on her husband's reaction. He disagreed so strongly with Resolution Nine that he threatened to leave the Seneca Falls Convention if it was read out loud. Later, when Elizabeth Cady Stanton read Resolution Nine at the Seneca Convention, her husband kept his word and left for the remainder of the convention.

A Success

The five organizers had no idea how many people would attend their convention. It was not well advertised. Only the one meeting notice had been published, and that had gone out just five days before the event. Mott cautioned that because it was

affecͭ thine
Lucretia Mott

Along with Elizabeth Cady Standon, Lucretia Mott (shown here) organized the Women's Rights Covention in Seneca Falls, New York.

haying time, "The convention will not be as large as it otherwise might be, owing to the busy time with the farmers, harvest, etc. . . ."[6]

The organizers arrived at the little church on Wednesday morning. They counted people waiting, with many more still arriving. Some dusty travelers had come by horse and buggy or wagon from as far as fifty miles away. The five women went to the door, but found it locked. Quick thinking solved this problem. Elizabeth Cady Stanton's nephew was lifted up to a window. He crawled through, unlocked the door, and hundreds of people crowded into the small building.

Over three hundred people in all, mostly women, came. Although the notice asked that only women attend on the first day, about forty men appeared. They, too, were welcomed.

After hearing speeches and discussing various issues, Elizabeth Cady Stanton read the Declaration of Sentiments. When papers were circulated for signatures, eleven of the resolutions passed unanimously. However, when Stanton read Resolution Nine, "Resolved, that it is the duty of the women of this country to secure to themselves their sacred right to the elective franchise,"—stating that women should have the right to vote—some of the convention-goers were shocked.[7]

Stanton held firm and pointed out that "the power to choose rulers and make laws, was their right by which all others could be secured. . . ."[8] After much debate, the resolution passed by a close margin.

At the end of the second day, sixty-eight women and thirty-two men signed the Declaration of Sentiments. Although the resolution for women's right to vote barely passed, it did become become part of the declaration. In her autobiography, Elizabeth

Cady Stanton declared the Seneca Falls Convention, "in every way a grand success."[9]

She was right. The Seneca Falls Convention "had set the ball in motion."[10] Yet newspapers across America ridiculed the Seneca Falls Convention. "All the journals from Maine to Texas seemed to strive with each other to see which could make our movement appear the most ridiculous."[11]

All the press coverage raised women's interest and inspired women like Emily Collins to fight for women's rights. Collins said:

> I was born and lived almost forty years in South Bristol, Ontario County—one of the most secluded spots in Western New York, but from the earliest dawn of reason I pined for that freedom of thought and action that was then denied to all womankind. . . . But not until that meeting at Seneca Falls in 1848, of the pioneers in the cause, gave this feeling of unrest form and voice, did I take action.[12]

Like Collins, more and more women (and men) began to accept and support the right of women to vote. Only twelve days after the Seneca Falls Convention, a second convention was held in Rochester, New York. There the resolution of women's right to vote was accepted immediately with no debate. Other conventions soon followed in Ohio, Indiana, Massachusetts, Pennsylvania, and New York City. Women's right to vote was accepted during all of those conventions.

The Seneca Falls Convention was the first of hundreds of women's conventions to be held over the next seventy-five years. When World War I started in 1917, many women began working outside the home. Many took jobs once held only by men. This and other national and world events forever changed the economic and social position of the American woman. These changes also forced men to reconsider women's voting rights. Within a few more years, through the efforts of many dedicated women, the Nineteenth Amendment would become law and give women the right to vote.

The United States Constitution: What Is It?

When the Seneca Falls Convention was held in 1848, the United States Constitution of 1787 was, and continues today to be, the highest law of America. This rather short document established the basic laws and principles under which America is governed. However, the Constitution was not written with women in mind.

The First Written Constitution

The 1776 Declaration of Independence guaranteed freedom for all Americans. It did not, however, give many rights to women. In the 1700s, some American women began to push for women's political rights—including the right to vote and the right to run for political office. During the writing of the Declaration of Independence, Abigail Adams advised her husband John Adams, "In the new code of laws which I suppose it will be necessary for you to make, I desire you would remember the ladies and be more generous and favourable to them than your ancestors."[1]

Abigail Adams's plea fell on deaf ears. John Adams (1735–1826), who later became the second American president, ignored his wife. In a May 26, 1776, letter to Massachusetts politician James Sullivan, John Adams wrote that women should not be allowed to vote:

> Because their delicacy renders them unfit for practice and experience in the great businesses of life, and the hardy enterprises of war. . . . Besides, their attention is so much engaged with the necessary nurture of their children, that nature has made them fittest for domestic cares.[2]

Five years later, the 1781 Articles of Confederation created a weak central government for all of the states. The government had limited power. For example, the new federal government could not collect taxes from the states. This meant it had no quick, reliable way of getting money. The Articles of Confederation did not establish a president or federal judicial (law-making) system. Without a strong central government and a president, relations and negotia-tions with other countries such as Great Britain and Spain were hampered. At that time, both Great Britain and Spain controlled large pieces of land in northern and western North America.

The young government struggled with its tasks and the states tried to unify as a nation during the 1780s. At this time, some Americans started to demand a stronger national government and constitution. Debates raged—should the Articles of Confederation be revised or should they be tossed out and a new con-stitution written? Dr. Benjamin Rush, James Madison, and George Washington represented those Americans who sought a new constitution.

Dr. Benjamin Rush (1745–1813) was physician general for the Continental Army during the

Revolutionary War. He strongly opposed the Articles of Confederation. On February 1, 1787, *American Museum*, a monthly Philadelphia magazine, published an article written by Rush called, "Address to the People of the United States." In it Rush wrote, "Most of the present difficulties of this country arise from the weakness and other defects of our governments."[3] Rush recommended forming a strong national government. He suggested various ways to accomplish this. Many of his ideas later became part of the United States Constitution.

Virginia native James Madison (1751–1836) became America's fourth president. He had read widely on the history of government. Before attending the 1787 Constitutional Convention in Philadelphia, he recorded in a notebook, "Vices of the Political System of the United States." There he listed his reasons explaining why America needed a new Constitution.

After serving as a general in the Continental Army, George Washington (1732–1799) retired in 1783. He returned to his Mount Vernon home. Over the next few years, he received alarming news of bankrupt Massachusetts farmers. They were rebelling against local courts that refused to give them debt relief. One farmer named Daniel Shays, a former captain in the Revolutionary War, was leading the rebellion. The armed farmers attacked state buildings and seriously injured lawyers, judges, and merchants. The state asked for help from America's Congress. Congress, however, had little money and few troops and could not send any aid. Finally, a Massachusetts militia defeated the rebels in Springfield. This rebellion became known as Shays' Rebellion.

Based on this and other events, George Washington decided that America needed a stronger federal government. In a November 5, 1786, letter to his friend James Madison, Washington wrote, "We are fast verging to anarchy and confusion!"[4] With a strong Constitution, he said, America would be restored to order during peacetime and would win the respect of other countries. Women's right to vote was not an issue raised by George Washington or any other male leader.

The Constitutional Convention

Urged by Madison, Washington, and others, the states agreed to a Constitutional Convention on May 14, 1787. Seventy-four delegates, all men, were chosen by their respective states to attend. Fifty-five went to Philadelphia, although only thirty-nine took a leading part in the discussions and the creation of the Constitution. The delegates agreed that changes were needed to strengthen the national government. Arguments soon erupted over whether to revise the Articles of Confederation or start over with a new Constitution.

Over the next few months, the delegates debated and discussed various plans. Those who wanted a stronger national government were in the majority. Their convictions finally led to a new Constitution.

The most influential delegate was probably James Madison. He drew on his extensive knowledge of government and political experience. Madison contributed many novel ideas about power and government. He recommended expanding the power of the national government and sharing the power between state governments, Congress, a president, and individuals. This meant that American citizens would elect their federal representatives. A federal judiciary, or legal system, and a two-branch lawmaking body—the House of Representatives and the Senate—would provide the checks and balances.

To keep the Constitution strong, Madison suggested adding amendments. Amendments could add new statements to the Constitution, change a particular portion of the Constitution, or nullify or repeal decisions made by the Supreme Court. These and other ideas of Madison's eventually became part of the United States Constitution.

The final plan at the convention called for a government with three branches or parts. There would be an executive branch, with a president and other officers, to run the government; a legislative branch, or Congress, to make laws; and a judicial branch with a court system and a Supreme Court at the top. Congress would consist of two parts: a House of Representatives and a Senate. Congress, made up of elected representatives, had the power to make the country's laws and raise taxes. Any suggested law, called a bill, must pass both the House and Senate. Then the law is sent to the president for approval. If the president signs the bill, it becomes law. If it is vetoed (not signed) then the bill goes back to the House and the Senate. They both must pass it by a two-thirds majority in order for it to become law.

On September 17, 1787, the Constitution was finished and read out loud to the delegates. Dr. Benjamin Franklin urged everyone to sign. Although he disagreed with several parts, he declared:

> On the whole, Sir, I cannot help expressing a wish that every member of the Convention who may still have objection to it, would with me, on this occasion doubt a little of his own infallibility and to make manifest our unanimity, put his name to this instrument.[5]

All but three of the delegates present signed.

Immediately, the Constitution was announced to the public. Now the new document had to clear a final hurdle—ratification, or official acceptance. According to Article VII of the Constitution, nine of the original thireen states had to ratify, or accept, the Constitution before it could become law. By June 21, 1789, nine states had ratified the Constitution. Some states, though, had agreed to ratify only if a Bill of Rights was added. The Bill of Rights, said these states, must protect the rights of individuals as stated in the Declaration of Independence.

Those Forgotten

At first, Madison was not in favor of a Bill of Rights. The Constitution, he said, protected all people under the law. Thomas Jefferson, though, explained that, "a bill of rights is what the people are entitled to against every government on earth."[6] Madison finally agreed with his friend. After Madison was elected to the House of Representatives, he began working on a Bill of Rights in April 1789. Madison's proposal was introduced into the House on July 21. Twelve amendments were sent to the states for ratification. Two were defeated. The remaining ten were called the Bill of Rights. They became part of the Constitution on December 15, 1791. These amendments give individuals many freedoms and protections such as freedom of religion, speech, and the press.

It took more than two years for the Bill of Rights to become law. Some bills can take many years to become laws. This is because more than twenty stages are required to move a propsal all the way through to an amendment. Much work is often needed on a bill. Briefly, here are the basic steps describing how a bill becomes a law:

1. A House member drafts a bill and gives it to the House Clerk. In this case, James Madison, a member of the House, drafted the Bill of Rights.

2. The House clerk gives the bill to the appropriate House authority, sometimes a subcommittee or committee.

3. The subcommittee considers the bill and may call in experts or hold public hearings. Such new information can sometimes cause the bill to return to the House, where it is discussed and changed.

4. Next, the revised bill comes up for debate in the House of Representatives. A representative can debate for up to one hour, although senators can debate as long as they want. All debates are recorded in the *Congressional Record*.

5. If the House passes a bill, it is sent to the Senate for more study, debate, and voting. Sometimes the House and Senate differ and will work together to resolve differences on a bill.

6. If both the House and the Senate approve the bill, it goes to the president, who signs it and makes the bill a law. The president can veto any bill, even one passed by both legislative branches. If this happens, the bill can still become law if two-thirds of both the House and the Senate approve it.

7. Amendments to the Constitution can come about in two ways. Congress, by a two-thirds vote in both the House and the Senate, can propose an amendment. Or a national Constitutional Convention can be held. To date, Congress has proposed all of the amendments added to the Constitution.

A proposed amendment must be approved by three-fourths of the states before it can become part of the Constitution. Congress can ask state lawmakers or state conventions to vote for ratification.

Even with the Bill of Rights, questions arose over whether the Constitution represented all Americans equally. Some said the Constitution focused on the federal government's role of protecting property and that it represented the views and experiences of middle-class and upper-class men only.

Most of the men who wrote the Constitution were free, white, wealthy property owners: lawyers, bankers, planters, merchants, and manufacturers. Nearly all had worked in the governments of their colony or state. Twenty had helped create the constitutions of their states. In those days, few Americans were well educated. Twenty-nine of the fifty-five delegates had college degrees, however. All together, these delegates brought a great deal of political experience to the Constitutional Convention.

Yet, according to Richard B. Morris, author and former history professor at Columbia University in New York, the delegates did not deal significantly with many different groups of Americans. These groups include slaves, debtors, paupers, Native Americans, and women. That is because most of these people:

> were not considered a part of the political [process.]
> True, the Founding Fathers [writers of the Constitution]
> held diverse views on the score of blacks, Indians, and
> women, but they managed to sidestep a direct
> confrontation on each of these . . . forgotten people—
> in numbers, a majority of the nation's inhabitants in
> 1787.[7]

Women were not allowed to vote after the United States Constitution was ratified. Over the seventy-five years following the Seneca Falls Convention, tens of thousands of women worked hard for suffrage. These women are putting up suffrage posters in New Jersey between 1914 and 1920.

✎ Women Cannot Vote

Historian Linda K. Kerber pointed out that the delegates to the 1787 Constitutional Convention, "shared assumptions about women and politics so fully that they did not need to debate them."[8] One assumption was that because women could not own property, they could not vote.

When the United States Constitution was written, most single women lived at home. They followed the rules of their fathers. When a woman married, she lived under the rule of her husband. A husband ruled or owned his wife and their house, land, and belongings. By law, married women could not own any property. Even their clothes and any earnings they made did not legally belong to them.

Women represented half of the American population. The writers of the Constitution and the Bill of Rights, however, made no account of women as a class. The delegates ignored women when they wrote the Constitution, said authors Doris and Harold Faber. This was not unusual explained the Fabers. "By doing so, they showed no special anti-feminist feeling. Throughout recorded history, the notion that women should have an active part in political life had rarely been taken seriously."[9]

Women are not mentioned in the Constitution. Instead, the Constitution discusses the rights of the people or persons of the United States. Only the president is referred to as *he*. This is the only place in the Constitution where a specific gender is mentioned. Under Article I Section 2, the Constitution sets no voting requirements. It says that each state can set the rules that qualify people to vote.

> Article I, Section 2: The House of Representatives shall be composed of Members chosen every second Year by

the People of the several States, and the Electors in each State shall have the Qualifications requisite for Electors of the most numerous Branch of the State Legislature.[10]

In their own constitutions, the states used the word *male* to limit voting to men only. To obtain the right to vote, women would have to persuade every state to remove male from their constitution or get an amendment added to the United States Constitution. The Seneca Falls Convention marked the beginning of this effort. Seventy-five years of hard work lay ahead before such an amendment finally became law.

3

Background of the Nineteenth Amendment

After the United States Constitution went into effect in 1787, women did not gain any rights. They still could not vote, sit on a jury, or run for political office. Married women could not keep any money they earned, make a will, or inherit or own property. Few women owned a business. Unskilled labor (as domestics in a wealthy home or at manufacturing jobs) was the only option for poorer women. Two professions were open to middle-class women: nursing and teaching. Women were paid much less than men in the same jobs, however. Women teachers earned 30 to 50 percent less than their male counterparts.[1] Furthermore, once a woman married, she generally gave up her job to become a full-time homemaker.

The 1848 Seneca Falls Convention stirred women across the country. Similar conventions were held every year except one in the twelve-year period between the Seneca Falls Convention and the Civil War. During these meetings, women voiced the need to change their legal and political status. They also demanded the right to vote.

Men reacted in various ways to the conventions. Some prominent men, including editor, journalist, and politician Horace Greeley, supported them. However, in the *Rochester Advertiser*, a New York newspaper, one man wrote, "To us they appear extremely dull and uninteresting, and, aside from the novelty, hardly worth notice."[2]

Other men and the majority of newspapers responded with ridicule and fury. An editorial in the Albany, New York, *Mechanics Advocate*, echoed the feelings of many.

> We are sorry to see that the women in several parts of this State are holding what they call "Women's Rights Conventions" and setting forth a formidable list of those Rights in a parody [ridiculous imitation] upon the Declaration of Independence. Every truehearted female will instantly feel that this is unwomanly. . . .[3]

As the Civil War approached, some women joined antislavery societies. They learned to organize, hold public meetings, and conduct campaigns. This helped them gain experience in politics. They would later use this power in their fight to obtain the right to vote.

The Civil War Years

Women put aside their demands for the vote during the Civil War, the war between the Union (the North) and the Confederacy (the South) from 1861 to 1865. Both northern and southern women raised money for the war and gave food and clothing to soldiers. Thousands became nurses and at least four hundred women, disguised as men, fought during the war. Others were spies, scouts, and couriers. Some women learned new trades such as printing and blacksmithing. Some were hired by the federal government, or worked in arsenals, factories, and textile mills. Many kept their family, business, or farm going while their men were away fighting.

Women everywhere hoped that their war efforts would help them obtain the vote. They were bitterly disappointed. They soon found that Congress and the public felt this was "'the Negro's hour,' and were not about to jeopardize citizenship and voting rights for African-American men by adding something so outrageous as votes for women," explained Edith Mayo, Curator of Political History at the Smithsonian Institution.[4]

After the Civil War

After the Civil War ended, the Equal Rights Association, a national organization, formed. Its members, both women and men, supported the three post-War Amendments—numbers thirteen, fourteen, and fifteen—to the Constitution. The Thirteenth Amendment, passed in 1865, abolished or ended slavery. The Fourteenth Amendment, passed in 1868, gave the vote to "male inhabitants" and "male citizens." With this use of the word *male* in the Constitution for the first time, women were again banned from voting. The Fifteenth Amendment gave African American men the right to vote for the first time in history.

As a result, in May 1869 two women's rights leaders, Elizabeth Cady Stanton and Susan B. Anthony, banded together and created the New York-based National Woman Suffrage Association (NWSA). Suffrage is another word for the right to vote. The NWSA wanted to get a federal or national women's suffrage law passed. Another suffragist group was formed in November of the same year. Led by Lucy Stone, Julia

Susan B. Anthony (shown here) worked tirelessly to get Congress to pass a woman's right to vote amendment to the United States Constitution. Elizabeth Cady Stanton and Susan B. Anthony formed the National Woman Suffrage Association.

Ward Howe, and Henry Ward Beecher, it was called the American Woman Suffrage Association (AWSA). AWSA worked for gradual adoption of women's right to vote on a state-by-state basis.

In 1870 the Fifteenth Amendment went into effect. With its passage, the vote could not be denied because of "race, color, or previous condition of servitude [slavery]." The Fifteenth Amendment did not mention women, however. They still could not vote.

The only real victories suffragists celebrated during this time were in the newly-settled frontier. Here, women were allowed to vote, first in the territory of Wyoming in 1869. When Wyoming applied for statehood in 1890, many in Congress opposed women's suffrage. They insisted that Wyoming repeal its law. The Wyoming Congress told the United States Congress, "We may stay out of the Union for 100 years, but we will come in with our women."[5] When Wyoming was admitted into the Union, it was the first state to give women the right to vote. During the celebration of its new statehood on July 23, 1890, Esther Morris, often called "the mother of woman suffrage in Wyoming," presented the flag honoring the occasion to the governor.[6]

Utah gave women the right to vote in 1870. That right was retained when it became a state in 1896. Idaho followed Utah's lead in 1896. Three years before, in 1893, Colorado women were allowed to vote. The Dakota territories gave women the right to vote in 1882.

Political Focus

During the 1870s and 1880s, women suffragists focused on political activities. They organized state suffrage associations, educated the public, conducted suffrage campaigns and speaking tours, and pressured Congress to pass an amendment to the federal Constitution. In 1871 and 1872, 150 women tried to vote in ten states and the District of Columbia. Few women had their votes counted. The most famous of these voting cases occurred when Susan B. Anthony led a small group of women to register, then vote, in the presidential election of 1872. Anthony realized that everyone involved was running a risk. Illegal voters could be fined up to $500 and imprisoned for up to three years.[7] She believed though that, "the fundamental right of citizenship, the right to voice in the government, is a national right."[8]

Two weeks after the election, Susan B. Anthony, her friends, and the three election officials who had allowed the women to vote were arrested. Susan B. Anthony was tried first. A jury trial for a criminal act is a right under the law. However, judge Justice Hunt, instructed the jury to find Susan B. Anthony guilty. He then fined her $100 and court costs. She refused to pay. Justice Hunt was worried that she might appeal to higher courts. So, he let her go free. Susan B. Anthony's friends never went to trial and President Grant pardoned the election officials. This case was discussed in newspapers across the country. The federal ban against suffrage remained in effect, however.

Suffragist leaders who went on campaigns and speaking tours were sometimes subjected to physical violence. Meetings repeatedly were stormed and disrupted. When Susan B. Anthony spoke in Albany, New York, the city mayor sat on the speakers' platform waving a revolver. This was meant to discourage possible attacks from the audience. Despite threats and mob violence, the women's suffrage movement continued to grow. It reached a high point in 1876.

Much excitement resounded throughout America that year—it was the centennial, or one hundredth birthday, of the United States. During May, Philadelphia was to host the first day of the country's largest celebration ever. It was called the Centennial Exposition. That same year, in January, the ninth annual convention of the NWSA began in New York City. Women were frustrated at not getting the vote. NWSA president Matilda Joslyn Gage expressed it this way:

Liberty today is . . . but the heritage of one-half the people, and the centennial will be but the celebration of the independence of one-half the nation. The men alone of this country live in a republic, the women enter the second hundred years of national life as political slaves.[9]

During the convention, NWSA members decided they would protest their lack of voting power during the Centennial Exposition. While Gage presided over the meeting, the women debated what action to take. Suddenly, the police appeared. They asked Gage to step outside the meeting hall. They told her she would be jailed unless she got a license for the meeting. Gage knew she did not need a license to hold a convention. She told the police that the United States Constitution guaranteed the right of people to assemble to discuss grievances or problems. This was the purpose of this NWSA meeting. Gage returned to her podium, told her audience what had happened, and the crowd loudly supported her actions. The police left.[10]

After forming their plan, some NWSA members traveled to Philadelphia to rent a place during the Centennial Exposition. When they finally found something suitable, only Susan B. Anthony could sign the rental agreement. Under Pennsylvania law at that time, married women could not make contracts. Anthony was the sole single woman in the group.

Soon after settling into its headquarters on Chestnut Street, the NWSA set up a suffragist materials library. They held many meetings and receptions to inform the public of their cause. Matilda Joslyn Gage and Elizabeth Cady Stanton worked separately, then together, on the Declaration of Rights of Women. This document expressed the desire for American women to have the same rights as men, including the right to vote. After its completion, the suffragists tried to get permission to present their Declaration of Rights on July 4, Independence Day. They wanted to do this during the huge Centennial Exposition celebration that was to be held in Independence Square. No matter what they tried, the women were denied permission. They then hatched a daring plan, one that could result in arrest and imprisonment.

On the morning of July 4, five NWSA members managed to get tickets for seats in the press section. This was close to where the grand ceremonies would take place. Meanwhile, thousands of people began crowding into Independence Square, waiting for the events to begin. First the Declaration of Independence was read to the crowd. Then Susan B. Anthony, Matilda Joslyn Gage, and the three other women, quickly walked to the stand. Susan B. Anthony handed Vice President Thomas W. Ferry a three-foot scroll tied with red, white, and blue ribbons. She said, "Mr. Vice President, we present this Declaration of Rights of the women citizens of the United States."[11]

Ferry, a supporter of women's suffrage, took the scroll and bowed. This ensured that the declaration would become part of the day's historic proceedings. The women left the stand. They tossed copies of the declaration along the way, and walked to an empty bandstand in front of Independence Hall. Here, Susan B. Anthony read the declaration out loud to a huge crowd. Then the NWSA, along with a large crowd, held a five-hour meeting.

Newspapers reacted to the Declaration in various ways, from silence to hostility to high praise. Many large New York newspapers either ignored the event or reported it incorrectly. Some Philadelphia newspapers carried positive articles on the event and reprinted the entire declaration.

Suffrage Gains

Even after this daring event, the suffrage cause slowed down. Historians Mari Jo and Paul Buhle explained why:

> Women simply lacked the power and influence to force the issue. The NWSA's congressional lobbying and the introduction of the 'Susan B. Anthony Amendment' in 1878 consequently produced no memorable political debate.[12]

Much of the opposition to suffrage came from various business groups. The liquor industry especially fought against suffrage. It did not want women to eventually pass laws regulating or stopping the sale of alcohol.

From then on, during every session of Congress, a bill for a women's suffrage amendment was presented but never passed. Public hearings on the amendment coincided with the annual convention of the NWSA in Washington. In January 1880, NWSA members spoke to the Committee on the Judiciary of the United States Senate. Julia Smith Parker, from Glastonbury, Connecticut, explained she wanted the vote because she paid "$200 a year in taxes without the least privilege of knowing what becomes of it."[13] Nancy R. Allen from Iowa was direct, "Equality of taxation without representation is tyranny."[14]

In the early 1880s, the movement received powerful backing from the Woman's Christian Temperance Union (WCTU). The union's young, new president, Frances Willard, brought hundreds of thousands of women into the NWSA. They were there to fight for suffrage as well as temperance, or a ban on alcohol sales. Few laws protected women and their children from drunken, abusive husbands and fathers. Stopping the sale of alcohol would help keep families safe. Willard led the WCTU for twenty years. She championed many reforms that would help women and children, including child labor laws, laws to protect working women, establishment of kindergartens, and women's right to vote.

In 1890 the Stanton-Anthony group merged with the Boston-based Stone-Beecher group. They formed the National American Woman Suffrage Association (NAWSA). For many years this combined association worked to advance women's rights on both the state and federal levels. Besides Stone, Anthony, and Stanton, leaders and supporters of the association included the noted American feminists Harriet Beecher Stowe, Julia Ward Howe, Clara Barton, Jane Addams, and Carrie Chapman Catt.

At Susan B. Anthony's insistence, Elizabeth Cady Stanton became NAWSA's first president and served for two years. Stanton left, though, when her growing interest in religion overlapped into the suffragist movement.

Suasn B. Anthony took the presidency next, until 1900. Throughout the 1890s, she mentored an assistant and close friend, Dr. Anna Shaw. This remarkable woman was first a teacher, than put herself through both theology school and medical school. Anthony saw Shaw as the next leader of NAWSA. Carrie Chapman Catt, however, showed her organizational talents, speaking abilities, and strong drive when she led a victorious campaign in Colorado for the woman's vote. Susan B. Anthony, now eighty years old, appointed Carrie Chapman Catt the third NAWSA president in 1900.

Catt quickly put a reorganization plan into place. Every state and territory was brought into NAWSA, even states without previous suffrage representation. Under Catt's leadership, Idaho gave women the vote in

1896. Catt also drew wealthy women to the suffrage cause. This helped bring money into NAWSA and allowed the organization to better carry out its work. After four years as president, in spite of her impressive gains, Catt resigned for several reasons. Her husband, who died a year later, was in poor health. Catt also was increasingly involved in the growing international suffrage movement. This was championed by Susan B. Anthony and Elizabeth Cady Stanton.

In 1904, Anna Shaw took over as NAWSA president. She held the position for eleven years, until 1915. Shaw was a gifted speaker. She did not, however, welcome differing ideas or approaches to the national organization. She often reacted negatively to them. Both her personality and ideas tended to irritate NAWSA officials.[15]

Suffrage Renaissance

During Shaw's presidency, NAWSA appeared not to develop and mature. Some historians call the years from 1896 to 1910 "the doldrums."[16] Other historians, such as Sara Hunter Graham, say this period represented a successful rebuilding of the suffrage movement. Its image became appealing to women from all walks of life. Writes Graham:

> Despite the poor record generated by state suffrage campaigns, however, the 'doldrums' were in reality an important period of growth and renewal for the movement. So significant were these years of regeneration that the period might be more appropriately called "the suffrage renaissance."[17]

During this time period, NAWSA began successfully recruiting middle-class and upper-class women as well as college-educated women. Many working-class women also joined the movement. The organization expanded its educational efforts. This included distributing literature to schools and libraries and sponsoring debates.

This building period coincided with many changes occurring for American women after 1900. More girls than ever were finishing public high school. Many worked at the increasing number of available office jobs. In mid   lass and upper-class families, females now had ca   nd further education choices. Many attended cc   female-only colleges or universities. Besides tr   al female careers such as teaching or nursing,   could become physicians, lawyers, dentists, and theologians. More training opportunities were now open to them. By 1910, 25 percent of all women over the age of fourteen were employed.[18]

New Ideas

At the beginning of the twentieth century, the idea of a federal suffrage amendment appeared dead. The state-by-state route of getting the vote just crept along. In 1908, only four states allowed women the vote: Idaho, Wyoming, Utah, and Colorado. By early 1913, women had full voting powers in nine states. In twenty-nine additional states, women could vote only on school, tax, or bond issues, or in city elections. The American suffrage movement was ready for change.

It came from several American women who had recently returned from England. These women, including Harriet Stanton Blatch, Alice Paul, and Lucy Burns, brought with them aggressive methods. Their activities violated the existing standards of what women could and could not do during this time period. The new suffrage leaders had learned such tactics while working with Emmeline Panhurst's suffrage group in England.

Panhurst was founder of the Women's Social and Political Union in England. She wanted Parliament to pass women's suffrage. Her group used militant actions to raise public awareness of suffrage. Panhurst's organization held parades and hunger strikes, disrupted national sports events, and carried out other actions that made suffrage front-page news.

Harriet Stanton Blatch, daughter of Elizabeth Cady Stanton, worked with Panhurst's organization in England. When she returned to America, she decided to breathe life into the suffrage movement. She formed the Woman's Political Union (WPU) in January 1907. Blatch explained why: "The suffrage movement was

Stump speaking—

In the days of "Old Dobbin" and Derby hats Mrs. Harriet Stanton Blatch exhorted the Wall Street crowds.

As seen on this newsreel footage, on Wall Street in New York City, Harriot Stanton Blatch, daughter of Elizabeth Cady Stanton, drew a huge crowd when she talked about women's right to vote.

in a complete rut in New York State at the opening of the twentieth century. It bored its adherents and repelled its opponents."[19]

By October 1908, Blatch's organization had nineteen thousand members. Many of them were working women. From her office in New York City, Blatch campaigned hard to convert state lawmakers to the suffrage cause. Thanks to her work, a suffrage bill was debated in both houses of the New York legislature. The last time the bill had surfaced was fifteen years before.

Blatch and her followers developed effective new ways of getting the suffrage message out. The WPU campaigned by trolley throughout New York state and by automobile in Illinois. Blatch held open-air meetings on behalf of women's suffrage. The last time such meetings had been run was thirty years before. The WPU also started large yearly parades of women marching down New York City's Fifth Avenue. Marchers carried yellow banners and wore yellow sashes that read "Votes for Women." During these parades, thousands of women would line the sidewalks. Houses along the parade route were decorated with yellow flags.

Blatch's methods made the suffrage cause newsworthy. Historian Ellen Carol Du Bois pointed out:

> The militant pursuit of publicity was an instant success: Newspaper coverage increased immediately; by 1908 even *The New York Times* reported regularly on suffrage. The more outrageous or controversial the event, the more prominent the coverage.[20]

Refocusing NAWSA

Alice Paul agreed with Blatch's methods. The youngest of the suffragist leaders, Paul returned to the United States from England in 1910. She spent two years completing a doctoral degree. She earned a Ph.D. in sociology in 1912 and worked with NAWSA under President Anna Shaw. However, Paul did not agree with NAWSA's focus on state suffrage campaigns. She tried to shift their focus to a federal constitutional amendment. Paul was joined by Lucy Burns. She was another young American who also had gone to England and been part of Panhurst's suffrage group. The two women agreed that the most direct way to get the vote for women was with a federal amendment to the Constitution.

In 1912, Paul and Burns offered to launch NAWSA on a renewed campaign for a federal suffrage amendment. Shaw agreed and Paul chaired NAWSA's Congressional Committee. Paul set her first big publicity plan to coincide with Woodrow Wilson's 1913 inauguration as President of the United States. Her plan was simple but controversial: to hold a huge parade of women, all marching for suffrage. Never before had such a large group of women, representing different suffrage organizations, banded together like this. Paul chose the day before Wilson's inauguration, March 3, for the parade. Many visitors from across America would come to Washington to see the inauguration the next day. This would be perfect timing.

Paul got a police permit for the parade so the marchers would have police protection during the event. It was quite unusual to see eight thousand women marching. Because of this, over half a million people lined the streets to watch the marchers, twenty-six floats, and ten bands. As the *Baltimore Sun* newspaper reported:

> The women had to fight their way from the start and took more than one hour in making the first ten blocks. . . .They suffered insult, and closed their ears to

jibes and jeers. Few faltered, though some of the older women were forced to drop out from time to time.[21]

The police failed to protect those in the parade, however. Mob violence broke out and the marchers were tripped, slapped, spat on or burned with cigars. Over two hundred people were treated for minor injuries at nearby hospitals. To protect the marchers, Secretary of War Stimson finally called out troops from nearby Fort Myer. Some of the marchers were congressmen and their wives. Because of this, an investigation was held and the chief of police for the District of Columbia lost his job.

Meantime, only a handful of supporters greeted Woodrow Wilson when he arrived in Washington, D.C. on March 3. When he asked where the people were, he was told they were watching the women's suffrage parade.[22]

Educating President Wilson

The parade and its investigation raised national interest in suffrage. This suited Paul just fine. One of her goals was to heighten awareness of the suffrage cause through publicity. However, she kept the Congressional Committee's focus on Congress. Only Congress could pass a constitutional amendment. To appeal to this group of lawmakers, Paul and her followers made and kept suffrage a major topic of discussion for President Wilson, political leaders, and the public. They did this through the use of various methods.

When President Wilson announced a special session of Congress on April 7, Paul brought three small delegations of suffragists to the White House during March. During the first delegation, Paul explained that women wanted Congress to consider suffrage right away. The President surprised the group and made national headlines when he replied "that Suffrage had never been brought to his attention, that the matter was entirely new. He added that he did not know his position and would like all information possible on the subject."[23]

Paul, of course, furnished the President with information right away. The Congressional Committee notified suffragists nationwide that a suffrage amendment would be introduced in the April session of Congress. Thousands of women wrote to the president. Groups of suffragists converged on Washington from all over the United States. The largest was an automobile procession to the Capitol on July 31. It handed Congress some two hundred thousand signatures on suffragist petitions. Because of Paul's tactics, Congress debated suffrage for the first time since 1887.

Meantime, in April 1913, Paul and Burns formed the Congressional Union. This national organization was formed to lobby Congress for a federal amendment. Anna Shaw welcomed this new organization as part of NAWSA. Paul and her followers continued to hold suffrage processions, pilgrimages, petitions, hearings, delegations, and public meetings.

Soon afterward, however, the Congressional Union and NAWSA split. Paul's group insisted all efforts go into a federal suffrage amendment campaign. NAWSA, instead, fought for state suffrage victories. The strategy of gaining the vote state by state worked in the West. There, women won in six states. It was not until 1913, however, that a state east of the Mississippi—Illinois—granted suffrage in presidential elections. Differences between the two groups grew so great that in 1914 the Congressional Union split off.

That same year, the Senate passed the women's suffrage amendment. Suffragists rejoiced until the House defeated it the next year. Anna Shaw resigned as NAWSA president in 1915. Carrie Chapman Catt resumed the presidency late that year. She pulled together the stagnating NAWSA and injected it with new tactics and organization.

Catt quickly developed a two-prong "Winning Plan" for a final drive toward suffrage victory. She requested that state leaders of the suffrage movement bury their differences and follow her directives. Then Catt asked each state to push for suffrage and to secure an amendment to the Constitution. Suffragists in states that had not adopted women's suffrage launched campaigns at once. Catt set up leadership training programs, schools for organizers, and conferences. She also created new fund-raising ideas. Suffragists in those states that had the vote helped others in states that did not. Catt also worked hard to convince President Wilson to support women's suffrage. A federal amendment that would require the president's support was also needed.

Under Catt's well-planned and organized leadership, NAWSA gained strength and direction. "The new group is taking hold and doing things splendidly . . ." said Anna Shaw, who supported Catt's leadership and ideas.[24] Catt described the revitalized NAWSA as, "A great army in perfect discipline moved forward toward its goal."[25]

Catt also realized that the idea of suffrage was gaining respect. Some two million suffragists were fighting for the vote daily. During one of her speeches, Catt declared, "There is one thing mightier than kings or armies, congresses or political parties—the power of an idea when its time has come to move."[26]

Both NAWSA and the Congressional Union had dedicated, talented members. Each also had members who donated large sums of money to the cause. Yet the two national organizations could not come together. They differed dramatically in their actions. NAWSA used personal lobbying and public pressure. The Congressional Union, which Paul renamed the National Woman's Party (NWP) in 1916, engineered direct, ongoing campaigns against the political party in power. The NWP's direct attacks resulted from President Wilson's public stand that although he favored suffrage, he wanted it won state by state. The sixty thousand NWP members backed Paul when she denounced the Democratic party, which was then in power, because Wilson did not support suffrage.

Some of the NWP's actions were light and fun such as one on Valentine's Day, 1916. That day the NWP gave one thousand suffrage valentines to senators, representatives, the vice president, and the president. Mr. Pou of the Rules Committee received a valentine with the following verse:

> *"The rose is red,*
> *The violet's blue,*
> *But VOTES are better*
> *Mr. Pou."* [27]

Representative Williams of the Judiciary Committee's valentine said:

> *Oh, will you will us well, Will,*
> *As we will will by you,*
> *If you'll only will to help us*
> *Put the Amendment through!* [28]

Militant Methods

The NWP's actions soon turned more militant. Paul went even further when she focused the NWP's actions directly against President Wilson. Blatch, Paul, and three hundred other militant suffragists met to plan action. They decided to post "sentinels of liberty" at the White House.[29] Starting on January 10, 1917, at 10:00 A.M., a dozen women with suffrage banners appeared in front of the White House gates. Two of the women held lettered banners.

One banner read:

MR. PRESIDENT WHAT WILL YOU DO FOR WOMAN SUFFRAGE?

The other read:

HOW LONG MUST WOMEN WAIT FOR LIBERTY?[30]

Silent picketers with banners remained at the White House gates for over eighteen months, every day except Sundays. They picketed in all kinds of weather—rain, snow, sleet, or sticky heat. On bitterly cold days, the women stood on hot bricks to keep their feet warm. On Wilson's Inauguration Day, one thousand suffragists joined the regular pickets. When the United States entered World War I (WWI) on April 7, 1917, the pickets continued. People reacted in different ways to the picketers.

Some ridiculed them. Others disliked the idea of women's suffrage, while still others applauded the NWP's actions. One Congressman heckled the picketers: "The other day, a man covered the gravestones in a cemetery with posters that read: 'Rise up! Your country needs you!' Now that was poor publicity. I consider yours equally poor."

"But," replied Nina Allender [NWP member], "we

are not picketing a graveyard. We are picketing Congress. We believe there are a few live ones left there."[31]

Paul, a Quaker, did not support the war. She said President Wilson denied American women the right to vote, but had brought the United States into WWI to fight for democracy. But, democracy should begin at home. During April and May, some people hurled insults and tomatoes at the picketers. The number of hostile onlookers grew. By June 1917, police were arresting the picketers because of riots that grew around them. At first the women got short sentences for obstructing traffic. Soon they received thirty-day and sixty-day sentences.

Picketer Ernestine Hara Kettler, then age twenty-one, remembered when she and the three other NWP picketers were given thirty days in the Occoquan, Virginia, workhouse. The women thought they had not done anything wrong. So, they refused to work. The biggest problem was the food. "It was just

To fight for suffrage, Alice Paul organized continuous pickets in front of the White House.

unbelievable—the worms that were found in the oatmeal we ate, in the soup we ate," Kettler said.[32] Some women tried to eat the bread, "if it wasn't totally moldy and if it didn't show rat tracks."[33]

The women soon went further. Many went on hunger strikes while in prison. After nine days, they were force-fed three times a day by tubes jammed down the throat or nose. They were also threatened with transfer to an insane asylum.

Picketers were treated with violence in jail and in the workhouse. Kettler remembered that other picketers, "were beaten and dragged across the patio from the superintendent's office to their cells . . . Some women had broken ribs and were bleeding profusely and they weren't treated. Others had all kinds of lacerations [cuts]."[34]

Newspapers across the country carried stories of this horrible treatment. Suffragist Laura Ellsworth Seiler recalled:

> I think everyone was just sort of nauseated over the whole thing; it was so horrible, such a dreadful thing for the women to go through. But I also felt that it was a very admirable and probably a very valuable demonstration. There's no doubt about it, her [Alice Paul's] effort is what precipitated the President's decision to bring the matter before Congress. [35]

Due to increasing pressure, President Wilson ordered all suffragists released from jail in 1918. Later, the Washington, D.C., appeals court ruled that the 218 jailed women had been illegally arrested and imprisoned.

Changes Come in 1917

Meanwhile, Catt and NAWSA were busy. NAWSA supported the war but pressed on with its suffrage work. Through Catt's efforts and the efforts of 2 million

NAWSA members, in six more states women gained a right to vote amendment by the end of 1917. New York, the most populous state in America, approved a full-suffrage amendment in 1917. Now the total number of full-suffrage states stood at eleven.

People
of the Time

Thousands of people worked on the suffrage cause during its seventy-five year battle. A handful rose to national leadership positions. Some of these people included Susan B. Anthony, Elizabeth Cady Stanton, Harriet Stanton Blatch, Lucy Stone, Alice Paul, and Carrie Chapman Catt. Many other women worked hard for suffrage. Because their contributions were less well known, however, we do not know much about them.

Here are profiles of two of those lesser-known suffragists. Laura Ellsworth Seiler developed into a public speaker for suffragist rights. Clara Ueland became President of the Minnesota Woman Suffrage Association (MWSA) and led Minnesota into a victorious fight for suffrage.

Speaking from the Streets

Laura Ellsworth Seiler was twenty-two years old when she first became involved with the suffrage movement. She marched in a successful suffrage parade up New

York's Fifth Avenue on May 4, 1912, along with ten thousand other women. According to an editorial in *The New York Times* about the marchers, some eight hundred men, representing nearly every trade and profession, participated in the parade. Seiler admired these men. "It took so much more courage for a man to come out for woman's suffrage than it did for a woman [back then]."[1] During the two-hour parade a huge crowd cheered or jeered the marchers, but no violence occurred.

After graduating from Cornell University in New York, Seiler joined the Women's Political Union (WPU). It was headed by Harriet Stanton Blatch. At the WPU's request, Seiler set out to organize two

Thousands of people came to watch colorful suffrage parades like this one held in Washington, D.C., on March 3, 1913.

counties in western New York State for suffrage. Seiler's mother came along as a chaperone. Before arriving, Seiler sent information about herself and the suffrage cause to the local newspapers. Once in town, she contacted people who were sympathetic to the cause. She helped them organize and launch local suffrage groups. The local group would then reach out to all the classes of women in the area and develop suffrage support. Seiler often made her street speeches in the early evening. This way, men could come after work to hear her.

After Seiler married she worked full-time as head of the WPU's Speakers Bureau. At this time WPU suffragists held demonstrations and spoke on street corners every night. They often stood on soapboxes to speak, while other suffragists passed out pamphlets. Other national suffrage organizations had their people speak only in rented halls. Seiler explained that "we believed that you had to get to the people who weren't in the least interested in suffrage. That was the whole theory."[2] Hecklers sometimes threw things, including stones, at the speaker, but no one ever received serious injuries.

Blatch created a steady stream of stunts to gain publicity. Seiler agreed with Blatch's policy:

> Mrs. Blatch's whole idea was that you must keep suffrage every minute before the public so that it gets used to the idea and talk about it, whether they agree or disagree. It must be something everybody was conscious of.[3]

Some of Blatch's publicity ideas were unusual. One morning Seiler was ordered to ride a horse in City Hall park and make a speech. She and the other speakers got there at noon, holding up traffic for quite a distance. The first woman's speech went fine.

senior, marched in the parade at the head of the student section. She wrote in her journal, "It's been a great day! I feel as if I have been a part in creating history."[5] Jones remained involved in politics. In 1942 she was elected president of the Minnesota League of Women Voters.

The well-received Minnesota parade and other suffrage events earned Ueland the respect of other suffragists. In 1914 she became president of the Minnesota Woman's Suffrage Association (MWSA). It later affiliated itself with the National American Women's Suffrage Association (NAWSA)

Ueland and her workers put together a series of fund-raising parties. Money was needed to carry out the MWSA's work and to pay full-time workers. Her ideas drew people and money. For example, one warm, muggy day in August 1915, a mix of fun activities was held at the Ueland's large home. Five hundred people attended. Men, because they were voters, had to pay fifty cents. Women paid only twenty-five cents. The activities included folk dancing, fortune-telling, a picnic supper, a play, and the sale of fruits, vegetables, jellies, and pickles. A new game called the Hoppetaria was a hit. Players hopped from one suffrage state to another on a game board, but had to skip nonsuffrage states or land on one foot on partial-suffrage states.

Ueland continually debated with men and women anti-suffragists, also called antis. Since 1876, the antis had formed their own organizations in twenty states. Their national membership, however, only hit a high of 360,000.[6] The antis declared that politics were for men and that women belonged in the home. Ueland countered by saying suffrage is "primarily a question of right and justice. Under republican form of government every one should have the right to a voice in the

Clara Ueland was the head of the Minnesota League of Women Voters.

laws they are forced to obey, irrespective of whether they desire to exercise that right or not."[7]

In 1915, Ueland lobbied Minnesota lawmakers for suffrage. She soon became the MWSA's chief lobbyist, displaying diplomacy and excellent listening and speaking skills. Her talents were not enough, however. Suffrage was voted down in the Minnesota Senate. Immediately, Ueland drew up a plan for a Minnesota suffrage victory in 1917. Minnesota suffragists traveled many long hours throughout the state. They organized local suffrage groups and trained people. Again, Minnesota lawmakers did not give women voting rights.

When War World I broke out, the MWSA assisted the war effort. It also maintained its stand and work on suffrage. Finally, in early 1919, House members voted 103 to 24 and Senate members voted 49 to 11 to allow Minnesota's women to vote in United States presidential elections. Later on September 8, 1919, Governor Joseph A. Burnquist called a special session. Its purpose was to vote for ratification, or acceptance, of the proposed federal suffrage amendment. This would give all women the vote. In less than thirty minutes, the House voted 120 to 6 for ratification. The Senate vote was 60 to 5 in favor. A radiant Ueland told everyone, "It is my happiest day."[8]

Later, Ueland became the first president of the Minnesota League of Women Voters. She died in 1927 at age sixty-six. Carrie Chapman Catt said:

> Mrs. Ueland was a heroine whose step never wavered when the torrent of opposition roared loudest. There never was a call to which she did not give quick study and sturdy response. That kind of oral courage is rare, and characterizes the great—the makers of history.[9]

5

Passing the Nineteenth Amendment

Following the influential state of New York's adoption of a suffrage amendment, the time was right for women to demand a constitutional amendment. Many factors acted together. As the number of suffrage states continued to grow, the number of congressmen accountable to women also increased. By 1917 the economic and social position of women was changing rapidly.

With the start of World War I, women joined the workforce in record numbers. They did work once reserved for men. They worked in aircraft, steel, machine-tool, high-explosives, textile and weapons factories, and drove ambulances. Others worked in brass and copper smelting and refining, and in oil refining. Women helped produce chemicals, fertilizers, and leather goods as well as railroad, automobile, and airplane parts. Thousands joined the military. Others nursed the wounded and knitted or sewed clothing for the soldiers. These changes made it increasingly harder to deny women the vote.

President Wilson's Stand

Carrie Chapman Catt again became NAWSA president in 1915. She began developing a program to win President Wilson's support of a federal suffrage amendment. Before he had become President, Wilson was anti-suffrage. After becoming President, he had moved through various phases. First, he felt he could do nothing unless his party acted on suffrage. Next he said he could do nothing until Congress acted on suffrage. Finally he declared that only the states could decide on the issue of suffrage. Unlike Alice Paul and her militant tactics, NAWSA president Carrie Chapman Catt felt that, "bringing him [President Wilson] to support of the federal amendment was a matter of time and tactics, and that he must on no account be personally antagonized or challenged on the issue."[1]

As an example of his support for those states deciding on the suffrage issue, just before the New Jersey bill on October 15, 1915, President Wilson told the newspapers he would go from Washington, D.C., to his hometown, Princeton, New Jersey. There he would vote in favor of state suffrage. Although he did vote in New Jersey, the President still would not favor a federal suffrage amendment.

During his 1916 reelection campaign for a second term as President, Wilson spoke at NAWSA's Atlantic City convention. He did not declare himself pro-suffrage, but he came close. He told the women:

> Almost every other time that I ever visited Atlantic City I came to fight somebody. I hardly know how to conduct myself when I have not come to fight anybody but with somebody. . . . We feel the tide; we rejoice in the strength of it and we shall not quarrel in the long run as to the method of it.[2]

Catt was convinced President Wilson had been won over to federal suffrage. His speech, she thought, was encouraging, although not definite. She noticed he never mentioned that it was the states' right to determine if women should vote, a previous theme he had brought up again and again.[3]

Within twenty minutes after the convention ended, suffragists had raised over eight hundred thousand dollars to fight for their cause. Within a week, following Catt's plan, four campaign directors and two hundred organizers were authorized to work for a federal suffrage amendment. State and national activities were coordinated. Afterward, Catt wrote to a friend, "I have put over the biggest week's work I ever did in all my life."[4]

The tide was turning for women. Jeannette Rankin, leader of the successful suffrage campaign in Montana, was elected to the United States House of Representatives. She took her seat in 1917 as the first woman in Congress.

The Fight Continues

Just before America entered World War I, Catt held a special meeting of her top people. They met to discuss NAWSA actions and war policy. By the end of the emotional meeting, NAWSA had written its war resolution:

> First, that the association should support the Government in case of war (a) by establishing employment bureaus for women, (b) by training women for agricultural work and elimination of waste, (c) by cooperation with the Red Cross. . . .

Second, that the first objective of the association should continue to be the submission of the federal amendment, and that war activities should not interfere with the purpose of the organization, which was obtaining the right to vote for all women.[5]

The third item established a three-woman team, including Catt, to communicate with President Wilson during the war. Catt understood the need for NAWSA to join in the national war effort. In this way, the suffragists could bring their case before the government and the public.[6] Newspapers across the country reported on NAWSA's resolution.

After the United States entered the war, NAWSA financed and managed an overseas hospital in France. Busy suffragists raised and canned food, made clothing, and volunteered with the Red Cross. They also established Red Cross chapters and sold over 4 million dollars' worth of bonds to raise money for the war. The last large New York suffrage parade was held on October 27, 1917. Women industrial workers, farmers, doctors, and nurses marched. Twenty-five hundred women marched while carrying cards that displayed over a million women's signatures for the suffrage cause.

Alice Paul's NWP refused to support the federal government in its war effort. To put pressure on President Wilson, Paul set up silent picketers to stand in front of the White House. The sayings on the banners differed, depending on current events.

The police began arresting the picketers. On October 20, 1917, Alice Paul was arrested for picketing. She was sentenced to seven months in jail. As she was taken to the patrol wagon, she shouted to onlookers:

> I am being imprisoned, not because I obstructed traffic but because I pointed out to President Wilson the fact that he is obstructing the progress of justice and

democracy at home while Americans fight for it abroad.[7]

Paul and another suffragist immediately went on a hunger strike, but both were force-fed.

From April to October 1917, Congress held a special war session to deal with the war effort. Suffrage was not discussed. When the sixty-fifth Congress opened on December 3, 1917, members again handled their usual work. The House of Representatives' Committee on Woman Suffrage recommended an amendment to give women the vote. The House of Representatives' Committee on Rules and the Committee on the Judiciary also recommended passage of the amendment.

However, the Committee on the Judiciary added a new section. This section stated that the amendment could not go into effect unless it was ratified by the states within seven years after its approval by Congress.[8] According to the Constitution, an amendment could not become law unless it was ratified by three fourths of the states.

NAWSA's annual convention was held in Washington, D.C., in mid-December, 1917. Six hundred members attended—a great turnout. This was the coldest December ever recorded. Many railroads had stopped running, and heating coal and food were scarce. Catt told those at the convention that she was losing patience with Congress. She declared:

> If the Sixty-fifth Congress fails to submit the Federal Amendment before the next congressional election, this association shall select and enter into such a number of senatorial and congressional campaigns as will effect a change in both Houses of Congress sufficient to ensure its passage.[9]

The *Women's Medical Journal* summed up the suffrage view this way:

> It would be an act of cold calculating wisdom for the men of America, as they enter the Great War [WWI], to give the women of America equal part in the government of the nation. Women should be given here and now, the vote, not as a bribe—thank God, they need no such incentive to effort and sacrifice—but as an aid to enlarge usefulness.[10]

The Great Debate

Debates over the suffrage amendment raged in the House of Representatives. On December 17, 1917, the Committee on the Judiciary recommended passage of the amendment and gave six reasons for the decision:

1. It is fundamentally just. The principle on which the American government was established—that governments derive their just powers from the consent of the governed—demands it. That woman is industrially and legally an individual. . . . Logic demands that she be a political entity as well.

2. The justice of the principle of woman suffrage has already been admitted in twelve States. Half a century ago it was proved that a democracy can not exist half slave and half free economically. It is clear it can not continue to do so politically.

3. Woman suffrage is inevitable. It is plainly written in the signs of the time. The only question is when and how.

4. The time for national action has come. . . . The passage of the Federal amendment would conserve the time and energy and money, not to mention the good will, spent in state campaigning and divert it to war service.

Carrie Chapman Catt spearheaded national and state campaigns that helped bring the right to vote to all women.

5. Never was there a time so fitted to passing this measure as now. Never was there a measure so suited to the times. Said President Wilson:

> We are fighting for the things which we have always carried nearest our hearts—for democracy, for the right of those who submit to authority to have a voice in their own government, defining our position in this world war. What better pledge of the sincerity of the purpose of the Government than to give to the women of the United States a voice in their Government—when they with the men of their country are giving all they have to make this principle safe throughout the world.

6. To limit the time allowed the several states for ratification of the amendment is to trip up justice by technicalities. When Congress has once endorsed the principle involved in the extension of the franchise to women it will defeat its own ends if it limits the legislatures in their procedures.[11]

On January 8, 1918, the House of Representatives' Committee on Woman Suffrage also recommended passage of a federal amendment. Its reasons included the following:

> Woman suffrage is no longer a controversial question; it is an established fact in nearly half the territory of our country. . . . With the overwhelming testimony on the one hand that woman suffrage in practice is a success and the unanswerable argument for the justice of woman suffrage on the other, there is nothing for a fair-minded American to do but to recognize the fact that woman suffrage is a sound principle in theory and in practice. With woman suffrage established as a sound principle, the only question remaining is, How shall it be written into the law of the land?[12]

The Committee on Woman Suffrage continued its discussions. There was talk of advances for women in other countries such as Great Britain, Canada, Mexico, France, Hungary, Italy, Sweden, Belgium, and Germany. Quotes from twelve state governors who fully supported suffrage were read. The recommendation ends with this paragraph:

> This crisis of our Nation [WWI], calls for bolder action than would have been necessary a year ago. We can not consistently profess to lead in a war for democracy and be the last nation to establish it at home. Nor can we claim that the Nation is fighting for democracy abroad and leave the States to demonstrate our understanding of democracy at home. The loyal votes of women who would vote in the places of absent men are a national concern. The war has made woman suffrage a national question. The Congress should treat it as such.[13]

A minority of the committee members voiced opposition to the amendment. On January 9, 1918, three members of the House of Representatives said they could not support the suffrage amendment. They believed that only the states can and should grant suffrage and only men should deal with politics. The three men quoted several national leaders including Thomas Jefferson and President Wilson.

Jefferson's quote was:

> All the world is politically mad. Men, women, and children talk nothing else, and you know that naturally they talk much, loud, and long. Society is spoiled by it. But our good ladies, I trust, are too wise to wrinkle their foreheads with politics. American women have the good sense to value domestic happiness above all other and to cultivate it beyond all other.[14]

They quoted President Wilson from October 7, 1915 who had said, "I believe that it should be settled by the States, and not by the National Government."[15] But President Wilson had changed his mind. On January 9, 1918, President Wilson told Congressman

Election Day!

This political cartoon captured a common anti-suffrage concern; if women got the vote, they would no longer want to stay at home and take care of the house and the children.

Judge Raker, chair of the House Committee on Woman Suffrage, that he now supported national suffrage. Congressman Judge Raker said to Catt that, ". . . when we sought his advice, he [President Wilson] very frankly and earnestly advised us to vote for the amendment as an act of right and justice to the women of the country and the world."[16] Catt's birthday on January 9 was made even more special when she heard this news.

Catt and other women across the country waited for January 10, 1918. This was the day Congress would vote on the suffrage amendment. The amendment would pass only if two thirds of Congress voted in favor of it. NAWSA had calculated that the vote would be close.

Congress Passes the Amendment

At 5:00 P.M. on January 10, 1918, the House of Representatives' clerk took roll call and recorded the vote of each representative. Up in the guests' galleries Catt and other NAWSA members kept careful record of the votes on their tally sheets. Some pro-suffrage voters came from the hospital to log in their vote: Sims of Tennessee came with a broken arm and shoulder. Mann of Illinois had been hospitalized for six months and was still too weak to stand for long. Barnhart of Indiana was carried in on a stretcher. Representative Hicks of New York came from his wife's funeral to vote for suffrage, before returning to her funeral. His wife had been a staunch suffragist.

The vote was announced, 274 in favor, 136 against. The suffragists in the gallery erupted in cheers. The roll call and voting were repeated twice, and the voting results remained the same each time. The amendment had barely passed by the required two-thirds majority. Catt thanked President Wilson for his support. The newspapers featured the House victory. They quoted Catt's prediction that, "the women of America will be voters in 1920, the one hundredth anniversary of the birth of Susan B. Anthony."[17]

In a remarkable coincidence, the British Parliament took a final vote on suffrage on January 10, 1918. Suffrage passed. Now women in Great Britain and Ireland could vote.

The United States Congress battle, though, had just started. Convincing the Senate to pass the amendment took all of 1918, half of 1919, and the election of a new Congress. In January 1918, Catt immediately swung into her action plan to convince anti-suffrage senators to change their minds. National newspapers ran editorials asking the Senate to vote yes to suffrage. Governors of suffrage states sent telegrams urging their senators to vote yes. Hundreds of suffrage resolutions poured into the Capitol. The Senate found and used an old law that banned printing petitions and resolutions to combat this.

Finally, the Senate set October 1, 1918, as the date to vote. The day before, President Wilson surprised the Senate members by asking them to pass the amendment. On October 1, the Senate vote was 62 for, 34 against. This was two votes short of the needed majority. The Senate defeated the suffrage amendment again on February 10, 1919, by only one vote. The suffragists now had to wait for the sixty-sixth Congress to start before another suffrage vote could be held.

Meanwhile, Alice Paul and the NWP declared that President Wilson was not doing enough for suffrage. Beginning in 1918, she organized new demonstrations at the White House. Some of the protesters were arrested and sent to prison.

President Wilson called the sixty-sixth Congress

into a special session on May 20, 1919. He was in Paris, France, involved with the aftermath of World War I. Wilson sent a telegram recommending that the House of Representatives and the Senate pass the suffrage amendment. That same day, the House voted and passed the amendment by a vote of 304 for, 89 against. At 5:00 P.M. on June 4, 1919, the Senate finally voted, 66 for, 30 against. This was enough to pass the Nineteenth Amendment.

Vice President Marshall signed the amendment with the "Victory Pen." NAWSA then placed the pen in the Smithsonian Museum in Washington, D.C. for all to see. President Wilson telegrammed congratulations to Carrie Chapman Catt from Paris.

The Final Fight

The final ratification battle was yet to be fought. This battle would involve all forty-eight states, because thirty-six states, or a three-fourths majority, was needed to ratify the suffrage amendment. Suffragist groups and anti-suffragist groups rolled up their sleeves to wage their biggest battle yet. Anti-suffragists used familiar arguments against the amendment, including the idea that suffrage would ruin women and destroy the home. Others said that "voting was unwomanly. 'I honor women too highly to allow them to descend into the dirty pool of politics,' one male politician said."[18]

Catt paid the anti-suffragist groups little attention. Within an hour after the vote in the Senate, she rolled out another well-organized plan for NAWSA. It needed to work the hardest in the anti-states of the East and South.

Both Catt and Paul sent telegrams to governors of all the states. They received encouraging responses. The New York and Kansas governors replied first, promising swift ratification. However, the first state to ratify the amendment was Wisconsin. Illinois was a close second and Michigan came in third. All three ratified the amendment on June 10, 1919. Six states ratified in June, three in July, two in August, and three more in September. The total now stood at seventeen.

The West, however, lagged behind in promises to ratify the amendment. To speed up the ratification process there, Catt and a group of campaign speakers took a train to South Dakota, Colorado, Idaho, Oregon, Utah, California, and New Mexico. They stopped in key cities along the way. The speakers urged suffragists to put pressure on their governors to ratify the Nineteenth Amendment.

Some governors gave excuses as to why they could not hold a special session. In Colorado, the governor said his budget would not allow it. NAWSA members offered to serve as clerical and file help to save expenses. The governor accepted the offer. Oregon's governor told Catt that:

> He was afraid that if he called a special session, the legislature would seize the opportunity to impeach him—a state of mind which was shared by another western governor. Both called the sessions, however, and lasted through them.[19]

After her exhausting six-week train campaign, Catt could now count on these states to ratify the amendment.

NAWSA's hard work paid off. By February 1920, thirty-three of the necessary thirty-six states had ratified the amendment. West Virginia became the thirty-fourth state to ratify, with Washington following a few days later. Connecticut and Vermont looked like they would ratify, but then their governors refused to call their lawmakers to a special session.

Eight states still had refused to ratify: Georgia, Alabama, South Carolina, Virginia, Maryland, Mississippi, Louisiana, and Delaware. Five states had not yet taken any action, including Tennessee.

In two states, Tennessee and North Carolina, a special session of the legislature was needed to vote for the Nineteenth Amendment. At first, Governor Thomas K. Bickeet of North Carolina announced he would call a special session on August 10. He made good on his promise. Three days later, however, he came out against suffrage and North Carolina voted against suffrage. Governor Bickeet urged the Tennessee lawmakers to vote the same way.

All eyes now turned to Tennessee—would this Southern state vote yes or no? If yes, then women of the United States could vote for President in the upcoming 1920 fall election.

Showdown in Tennessee

By August 1920, only one more state was needed to ratify the suffrage amendment. So far, the thirty-four states listed in the chart on page 74 had ratified the amendment.

Thanks to a telegram from President Wilson, Tennessee Governor Albert H. Roberts agreed to hold a special session of his state's lawmakers in August 1920. Catt arrived in the state capital, Nashville, before then. She launched into a grueling speaking tour of the larger cities in Tennessee. Catt's tour and speeches were reported in large and small newspapers across the country. In the mountains of east Tennessee, in a small village called Niota, a mother followed the suffrage news with great interest. Recently, her twenty-four-year-old son Harry Burn had been elected to his first term in the House of Representatives. Mrs. Febb King

Ratifying the Suffrage Amendment

Year	Month	States	Number of States
1919	June	Illinois, Michigan, Wisconsin, New York, Kansas, Ohio, Pennsylvania, Massachusetts,	8
	July	Iowa, Missouri, Arkansas	3
	August	Montana, Nebraska	2
	September	Utah, Minnesota, New Hampshire	3
	November	California, Maine	2
	December	North Dakota, South Dakota, Colorado	3
1920	January	Rhode Island, Indiana, Kentucky, Oregon, Wyoming	5
	February	Nevada, New Jersey, Idaho, Arizona, New Mexico, Oklahoma	6
	March	West Virginia, Washington	2
			TOTAL 34

Ensminger Burn had made her son Harry "promise that, when he went to the special session, if his vote were needed for ratification he would give it."[20]

The Tennessee Senate quickly ratified the amendment on August 13—twenty-five votes for, four against. In its report, the Senate wrote:

> National wom[e]n's suffrage by Federal Amendment is at hand; it may be delayed, but it cannot be defeated; and we covet for Tennessee the signal honor of being the thirty-sixth and last State necessary to consummate this great reform.[21]

Now it was up to the Tennessee House of Representatives. Anti-suffragists had been pressuring the House members not to let the amendment pass. Meantime, Mrs. Febb King Ensminger Burn, at home in Niota, had been following the newspapers. She sent a letter to her son, reminding him of his promise:

> *Dear Son:*
> *Hurrah and vote for suffrage! Don't keep them in doubt. I notice some of the speech against. They were bitter. I have been watching to see how you stood, but have not noticed anything yet. Don't forget to be a good boy and help Mrs. Catt put 'rat' in ratification.*
>
> *Your Mother.*[22]

On August 18, the House voted, but the suffrage amendment was two votes short. When the vote was taken again, a pro-suffrage representative had arrived from a hospital to vote. This time, the voting result was a tie. Representative Banks Turner had changed his mind and voted for the amendment. With ninety-six members present, the vote was 48 to 48. A tie meant that a new vote was necessary.

Just one more vote was needed for the tiebreaker. Again the House members voted. When the clerk said the name of Harry Burn, the young lawmaker remembered his promise to his mother and called out, "Aye! The whole House broke into an uproar that was heard outside for blocks around."[23] Then the entire House chamber, members and guests, broke into a spontaneous hymn of praise.

Later when questioned, Burn said:

[I voted] in favor of ratification first, because I believe in full suffrage as a right; second, I believe we had a moral and legal right to ratify; third, I knew that a mother's advice is always safest for a boy to follow, and my mother wanted me to vote for ratification; fourth, I appreciated the fact that an opportunity such as seldom comes to a mortal man to free seventeen million women from political slavery was mine; fifth, I desired that my party in both state and nation might say that it was a Republican from the mountains of East Tennessee . . . who made national woman suffrage possible and this date, not for personal glory but for the glory of his party.[24]

There is a postscript to Harry Burn's famous vote. Soon after Burn explained his suffragist vote at the House of Representatives, his mother sent him a telegram. An anti-suffragist had tried to get Mrs. Burn to say that her suffragist letter to Harry was a fake. Her telegram read:

Woman was here today, claims to be the wife of Governor of Louisiana and secured an interview with me and tried by every means to get me to refute and say that the letter I sent to my son was false. The letter is authentic and was written by me and you can refute any statement that any party claims to have received from me. Any statement claiming to be from me is false. I stand squarely behind suffrage and request my son to stick to suffrage until the end. This woman was very insulting to me in my home and I had a hard time to get her out of my home.[25]

After the governor of Tennessee signed the ratification certificate, he sent it by registered mail to Washington, D.C. The secretary of state's office received it at 4:00 A.M. on August, 26, 1920. After the certificate was certified to be correct, Secretary of State Bainbridge Colby signed the Proclamation of the Women's Suffrage Amendment to the United States Constitution. The only witness present was his own secretary. On that day, August 26, 1920, the Nineteenth Amendment officially became law in the United States.

Secretary Colby had invited Carrie Chapman Catt to witness the signing. She came a bit later after the signing, along with Harriet Taylor Upton, who had worked hard for suffrage in Ohio, and Maud Wood Park. Park recalled, "We almost had to stick pins in ourselves to realize that the simple document at which we were looking was . . . the long sought chapter of liberty for the women of this country."[26] At the State Department, Secretary Colby read the new law to Catt and other suffragists. Catt and one of her aides then went to the White House to thank President Wilson for his help.

As news of the Nineteenth Amendment spread, bells rang, whistles blew, and politicians congratulated suffragists across the United States. In Washington, D.C., Alice Paul sewed star number thirty-six, the last star, onto her suffrage banner and hung it from the NWP headquarters balcony. That same night, Catt spoke at a huge celebration party at a Washington, D.C., theater. Secretary Colby read the following message from President Wilson:

I deem it one of the greatest honors of my life that this

great event, so stoutly fought for, for so many years, should have occurred during my administration. Nothing has given me more pleasure than the privilege of doing what I could to hasten the day when the womanhood of the nation would be recognized on the equal footing it deserves.[27]

6

Immediate
Ramifications

On August 18, 1920, when the Nineteenth Amendment was ratified by a three-quarters majority of the states, 26 million Americans—about 52 percent of the population—became full-fledged citizens of the United States.[1] Magazines began to run many articles about the "New Woman." Writers of these articles, along with many Americans, assumed that the new amendment brought women full rights as citizens and that women were now part of the politics.[2]

While the vote was crucial, the law still treated women differently from men in many situations. Women were still banned from jury duty. They also could not run for or hold political office. They still did not receive the same pay as men for the same work. They could not inherit or will property. They could not work at some jobs because of their gender. Finally, if they married a man from a country outside the United States, they lost their American citizenship. More hard work by various women's organizations was ahead.

Equal Rights Amendment

Once the vote was won, Alice Paul and her organization, the National Women's Party (NWP), tackled issues of the working woman. The NWP began to lobby for another amendment for equal pay between men and women doing the same job. They called it the Equal Rights Amendment (ERA) or the Lucretia Mott Amendment. A final draft was approved at Seneca Falls in July 1923. This was the site of the first women's rights convention. That month also marked the seventy-fifth anniversary of this historic event.

The NWP wrote the amendment to give full citizenship and full equality to women. It said, "Men and women shall have equal rights throughout the United States and every place subject to its jurisdiction. Congress shall have the power to enforce this article by appropriate legislation."[3] On December 10, 1923, the nephew of Susan B. Anthony, Congressman Daniel Anthony, introduced the amendment in the House of Representatives and three days later the Senate began debating it. It did not pass.

Birth of the National League of Women's Voters

In contrast, Carrie Chapman Catt, head of NAWSA, focused on how women would learn to use their vote once they got it. Most women had little experience in politics up to this time. They needed to learn how the political system worked and how to be part of it. Back in late March 1919, at NAWSA's fiftieth anniversary in St. Louis, Missouri, Catt had proposed:

> As a fitting memorial to a half century of progress, the association invites the women voters of the fifteen full suffrage states to attend this anniversary and there to join their forces in a League of Women Voters, one of

whose objects shall be to speed the suffrage campaign in our own and other countries.[4]

She recommended that the league be free from religious or racial bias. It also needed to work to free women from legal discrimination, and to launch a program of political education and leadership. She also suggested that schools teach citizenship to both girls and boys. Because the league would be the first of its kind, a five-year trial would determine the success of this new organization. Convention-goers agreed and the National League of Women Voters (NLWV) was formed as part of NAWSA. It became independent a year later, and later changed its name to the League of Women Voters (LWV).

Catt concentrated on getting women out to vote. A final resolution from NAWSA declared:

> Whereas millions of women will become voters in 1920 and whereas the low standards of citizenship found among men clearly indicate the need of education in the principles and ideals of our government and methods of political procedures, therefore be it resolved, that the National League of Women Voters be urged to make political education of the new women voters (but not excluding men) its first duty in 1920.[5]

To help women learn about the political process, NLWV set up citizenship schools. It showed women how to mark voting ballots. Just before the presidential election, NLWV members telephoned women to remind them to vote. On the 1920 presidential election day, NLWV members babysat, and drove women to and from the polls. Twenty million women were now eligible to vote, but only 37 percent of the women nationwide voted.[6]

For those who did vote, many recognized the historical significance of the event. One of the new voters in the presidential election was Charlotte Woodward. She was over ninety years old. She recalled when she had attended the 1848 Seneca Falls Convention. Woodward had traveled in a family wagon in upstate New York. She said:

> At first we traveled quite alone under the overhanging tree branches and wild vines, but before we had gone many miles we came on other wagonloads of women, bound in the same direction. As we reached different crossroads, we saw wagons coming from every part of the country, and long before we reached Seneca Falls we were a procession. . . .[7]

When twenty-year-old Ann Salsberg heard that the Nineteenth Amendment had been ratified, she immediately rushed to Camden, New Jersey, to register to vote. She wanted to be the first local woman to register. She recalled that the men there were not ready for her. "The all-male staff huddled together," she said. "What should they do? Finally, one said, 'Go on and let her register. She'll be a good Republican.'"[8]

Woodward and Salsbery were part of the procession of women who voted in 1920. Many historians agree, however, that this presidential election "was a tremendous disappointment. Women had worked so long for the vote and called the ballot the most precious privilege of a free society. . . . But most did not vote."[9]

During local and state elections the following year, once again, most women did not vote. Part of the reason was that "women, except for one or two hardy spirits, were too timid to participate in an election where men folks made it plain they were not wanted," reported the Minnesota chapter of the NLWV.[10]

NLWV Tries Harder

During spring 1921, Catt called a final meeting of NAWSA. Catt gave a speech that included these words:

> As I look back over our years of work together, there is nothing thrilling about them. It was just long, grilling, unceasing, hard labor. Future historians perhaps may make heroines out of some of us, for it is true that many women have given their entire lives to our cause.[11]

Meantime, the NLWV continued to encourage women to participate in politics. Members printed election pamphlets that described candidates. Pamphlets were distributed to men and women. Later, the organization started an education program and political reform programs. These showed women how to use political power to deal with zoning, revitalization of poor neighborhoods, and school changes.

Even fewer women voted in 1922. There was no presidential vote that year. Sixteen women ran for Congress. Only one won, Winifred Mason Huck of Illinois. She finished the term of her father, who had died while in Congress. Another woman, Anna Dickie Olesen, was the first woman from Minnesota to run for the United States Senate. To appeal to those who questioned her capabilities because of her gender, Olesen told voters, "I ask no consideration because I am a woman. I also ask that no one close his mind against me because I am a woman."[12] Although Olesen offered voters much political experience and savvy, she lost.

A Decade of Change

During the 1920s, many women's organizations that had started during the suffragist years continued their work for reforms, particularly for women and children. These organizations, including the NLWV, carried on the work of NAWSA, together established the Women's Joint Congressional Committee (WJCC) in 1920. The WJCC worked "as a clearinghouse for the federal legislative efforts of the affiliated organizations."[13] The greatest success of the WJCC was the short-lived 1921 Sheppard-Towner law. It gave federal money to health care programs for mothers and children. It was also the federal government's first attempt into social welfare law. Eventually forty-five states accepted it, but it was automatically repealed (reversed) on June 30, 1929. Much of the law's death was due to American's fear of socialism and communism.[14]

The Equal Rights Amendment became the sole focus of the NWP. However, the NLWV and other women's organizations "believed that the amendment would endanger legislation protecting women

Carrie Chapman Catt addresses an early League of Women Voters committee in the 1920s.

workers, which they had struggled so vigorously to see implemented."[15]

By gaining the vote, women began to slowly make inroads into the political and working world of men. More women started working outside the home in the 1920s. The female labor force grew by 26 percent during this time.[16] Most married women, though, worked in their homes. In fact, from 1920 to 1940 about 75 percent of women worked as homemakers while 25 percent worked at paying jobs outside the home.[17] Once the United States entered World War II (1939–1945) in 1941, the number of women holding jobs outside the home skyrocketed.

After women got the vote, they did not form political parties of their own but voted along the established party lines. They frequently echoed their husband's voting decision. More often than not, they just did not vote. During an interview, suffragist Laura Ellsworth Seiler recalled that many of her friends were indifferent about women getting the vote.

> Most of my friends said, "This isn't going to make any difference; they're going to vote the way their fathers and theirs husbands do anyway". . . . As it happened, that's just about the way it turned out, unhappily.[18]

Small victories were noted. A decade after winning the right to vote, the NLWV announced that two women had served as state governors. One hundred forty-six women had been elected to lawmaking bodies, thirteen were representatives in the House, and one was in the Senate. By 1927 in Minnesota, for example, 204 women had been elected to county and city offices.[19] This included county and city offices, positions as superintendents of schools, and positions as village, town, and city clerks. Men still far outnumbered women in political offices, however.

They also still controlled business and professions such as medicine, law, and dentistry.

Too many women did not understand how the political system worked. Suffragist Laura Ellsworth Seiler summed up this issue, "At that time, I think it hadn't occurred to a great many women that once they got the vote, the rest wouldn't be easy. I think most men felt that."[20]

The editor of the *Ladies Home Journal* magazine wrote that during the 1920s, women:

> Had made little difference in the parties or the quality of office holders because 1928 was really the first year women began to be alive to political questions and play a substantial part in the election. Many thought that [Herbert] Hoover owed his election [in 1928] to the women's vote.[21]

Not until 1936 did more than half of the women vote.[22] It has taken time—much more than one decade—for women to gradually change many of the old laws and social conditions and gain new liberties and rights.

Getting the vote has been an important first step in this process of change.

How the Nineteenth Amendment Affects Us Today

Women have come a long way since the ratification of the Nineteenth Amendment in 1920. Political equality with men is still an issue, however.

Equal Rights Amendment

Since it was first created in 1923, an Equal Rights Amendment proposal was introduced in every session of Congress until 1972. In 1943, the wording of the proposed ERA was changed to conform to other constitutional amendments. The ERA then read, "Equality of Rights under the law shall not be denied or abridged by the United States or by any State on account of sex."[1]

During the early 1970s, many women's organizations such as the National Organization for Women (NOW), the Women's Political Caucus, the National League of Women's Voters (NLWV), and others worked hard to pass the amendment. In March 1972 Congress passed the ERA and sent it to the states to be ratified by 1977. By late 1977, thirty-one states had ratified the ERA. Only seven more states were needed for ratification.

Opposition to the ERA continued to increase. Yet, according to Edith Mayo, a retired Smithsonian Institution curator:

> Supporters lobbied, petitioned, and staged parades and demonstrations successfully extending the deadline to pass the ERA to 1982. By the end, opponents of the ERA were more successful in frightening the public about the supposed destruction of the family and the end of women's role in the home than its supporters were in convincing the public of the ERA's benefit.[2]

The ERA proposal died in 1982, without a majority of votes in favor. Since then, the ERA has been re-introduced into Congress but has never passed again. To sum up the battle over the ERA, Edith Mayo wrote, "Women are still divided over the need for the ERA, but continue to seek equal protection under the law."[3]

Women's Voting Power

American women have become much more involved in politics since the 1980s. In 1980, for the first time, women voters outnumbered men voters in presidential elections. Women have outnumbered men voters in non-presidential elections since 1986. Higher percentages of women then men also register to vote.[4] This has forced the candidates to pay attention to issues of particular interest to women such as domestic violence, sexual assault, and equal pay. Colorado Representative Pat Schroeder believes that, "Women are finally coming to understand that it is politics that affects many of these quality of life issues, and to affect politics you must vote."[5]

In 1981, Sandra Day O'Connor was named by President Ronald Reagan as the first woman Justice on the United States Supreme Court. She filled the vacancy created by the retirement of Justice Potter Stewart.

As a result of women becoming more involved in voting and politics, "Our government policies have become friendlier and fairer to women, more responsive to the people who have to deal with the concerns of running a family and keeping a community going," said Illinois Senator Carol Moseley-Braun, the first African-American woman ever elected to the Senate.[6]

With more women in Congress, more bills on women's issues and families have been passed. Since the 1990s, dozens of new laws that affect women have

Making her first speech in Congress in May 1917, Jeanette Rankin, first female member of Congress, paved the way for other women to enter politics.

been passed. Perhaps the most significant one was the Family and Medical Leave Act. Since 1990, congresswomen have helped channel money into research for breast cancer, a leading killer of women. Senator Kay Bailey Hutchison from Texas stated that, "When you look at the issues we tackle in Congress today that affect women, you just have to appreciate that none of this would have happened unless we had the right to vote."[7]

Women favored President Bill Clinton over opponent Bob Dole by 17 percentage points in the 1996 presidential election.[8] Clinton may have garnered such strong support because he appointed women to 27 percent of the positions that require Senate confirmation during his first term from 1992 to 1996.[9] With this percentage, Clinton set a White House record compared to past Presidents. In 1996, President Clinton appointed Madeleine Albright as Secretary of State, making her the highest ranking female to hold a United States government office.

Still, the United States has never had a female president. Other countries have had female leaders, including Great Britain's Margaret Thatcher and Israel's Golda Meir. Political history was made in 1984 when Walter F. Mondale ran for President and chose Geraldine Ferraro, the first woman candidate for vice president, as his running mate. They lost the election, however. According to Marilyn Lewis, a newspaper journalist, this "is a visible sign that, despite progress in integrating the labor force, few women have penetrated the nation's centers of power."[10]

Suffrage Remembered

In 1995 special events celebrating the seventy-fifth anniversary of the Nineteenth Amendment were held across the United States. The League of Women Voters, headquarted in Washington, D.C., prepared a traveling exhibit on the impact of the women's vote. In mid-July Seneca Falls, New York, held several events. A suffrage parade following the same route suffragists took when they demonstrated in the capital, and a reenactment of the 1848 convention were featured.

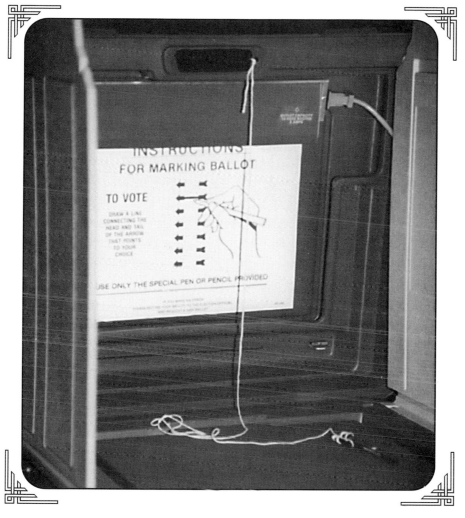

In the past, voters filled out a slip of paper and dropped their vote into a wooden box. Today, voters use a private voting booth like this one.

The federal government joined in, too. The Postal Service issued a colorful first-class stamp to commemorate the seventy-fifth anniversary of the Nineteenth Amendment. The National Archives in Washington, D.C., which houses the Constitution and amendments, hosted a ratification party.

After seventy-five years, lawmakers voted to move a marble statue of Elizabeth Cady Stanton, Susan B. Anthony, and Lucretia Mott—three leading women in the suffragist movement—from the lower level of the United States Capitol to its rightful site, the United States Capitol Rotunda. The nine-ton statue is now visited by over 4 million people each year. The statue was commissioned by the National Woman's Party after the Nineteenth Amendment passed in 1920 to honor Stanton, Mott, and Anthony. These three leaders fought most of their lives for the vote, but died before seeing the amendment become law.

Historian and author Robert Cooney believes that women's suffrage and the Nineteenth Amendment represent an American triumph.

> The women's suffrage movement stands as a lasting affirmation of our country's democratic promise, for it re-emphasizes the importance of the most fundamental democratic value, the right to vote. The suffrage movement holds a particular relevance now. It celebrates rights of women and honors those who helped win them. It is both a lesson of history suppressed and misunderstood and a lesson of history triumphant.[11]

THE CONSTITUTION OF THE UNITED STATES

The text of the Constitution is presented here. All words are given their modern spelling and capitalization. Brackets [ ] indicate parts that have been changed or set aside by amendments.

Preamble

We the people of the United States, in order to form a more perfect Union, establish justice, insure domestic tranquility, provide for the common defense, promote the general welfare, and secure the blessings of liberty to ourselves and our posterity, do ordain and establish this Constitution for the United States of America.

ARTICLE I
The Legislative Branch

Section 1. All legislative powers herein granted shall be vested in a Congress of the United States, which shall consist of a Senate and House of Representatives.

The House of Representatives

Section 2. (1) The House of Representatives shall be composed of members chosen every second year by the people of the several states, and the electors in each state shall have the qualifications requisite for electors of the most numerous branch of the state legislature.

(2) No person shall be a representative who shall not have attained the age of twenty-five years, and been seven years a citizen of the United States, and who shall not, when elected, be an inhabitant of that state in which he shall be chosen.

(3) Representatives and direct taxes shall be apportioned among the several states which may be included within this Union, according to their respective numbers, [which shall be determined by adding to the whole number of free persons, including those bound to service for a term of years, and excluding Indians not taxed, three-fifths of all other persons]. The actual enumeration shall be made within three years after the first meeting of the Congress of the United States, and within every subsequent term of ten years, in such manner as they shall by law direct. The number of representatives shall not exceed one for every thirty thousand, but each state shall have at least one representative; [and until such enumeration shall be made, the state of New Hampshire shall be entitled to choose three, Massachusetts eight, Rhode Island and Providence Plantations one, Connecticut five, New York six, New Jersey four, Pennsylvania eight, Delaware one, Maryland six, Virginia ten, North Carolina five, South Carolina five, and Georgia three].

(4) When vacancies happen in the representation from any state, the executive authority thereof shall issue writs of election to fill such vacancies.

(5) The House of Representatives shall choose their Speaker and other officers; and shall have the sole power of impeachment.

The Senate

Section 3. (1) The Senate of the United States shall be composed of two senators from each state, [chosen by the legislature thereof,] for six years; and each senator shall have one vote.

(2) Immediately after they shall be assembled in consequence of the first election, they shall be divided as equally as may be into three classes. The seats of the senators of the first class shall be vacated at the expiration of the second year, of the second class at the expiration of the fourth year, and of the third class at the expiration of the sixth year, so that one-third may be chosen every second year; [and if vacancies happen by resignation, or otherwise, during the recess of the legislature of any state, the executive thereof may make temporary appointments until the next meeting of the legislature, which shall then fill such vacancies].

(3) No person shall be a senator who shall not have attained to the age of thirty years, and been nine years a citizen of the United States, and who shall not, when elected, be an inhabitant of that state for which he shall be chosen.

(4) The Vice President of the United States shall be president of the Senate, but shall have no vote, unless they be equally divided.

(5) The Senate shall choose their other officers, and also a president *pro tempore*, in the absence of the Vice President, or when he shall exercise the office of President of the United States.

(6) The Senate shall have the sole power to try all impeachments. When sitting for that purpose, they shall be on oath or affirmation. When the President of the United States is tried, the Chief Justice shall preside: and no person shall be convicted without the concurrence of two-thirds of the members present.

(7) Judgement in cases of impeachment shall not extend further than to removal from office, and disqualification to hold and enjoy any office of honor, trust, or profit under the United States: but the party convicted shall nevertheless be liable and subject to indictment, trial, judgement and punishment, according to law.

Organization of Congress

Section 4. (1) The times, places and manner of holding elections for senators and representatives, shall be prescribed in each state by the legislature thereof; but the Congress may at any time by law make or alter such regulations, [except as to the places of choosing senators].

(2) The Congress shall assemble at least once in every year, [and such meeting shall be on the first Monday in December], unless they shall by law appoint a different day.

Section 5. (1) Each house shall be the judge of the elections, returns and qualifications of its own members, and a majority of each shall constitute a quorum to do business; but a smaller number may adjourn from day to day, and may be authorized to compel the attendance of absent members, in such manner, and under such penalties as each house may provide.

(2) Each house may determine the rules of its proceedings, punish its members for disorderly behavior, and, with the concurrence of two-thirds, expel a member.

(3) Each house shall keep a journal of its proceedings, and from time to time publish the same, excepting such parts as may in their judgement require secrecy; and the yeas and nays of the members of either house on any question shall, at the desire of one-fifth of those present, be entered on the journal.

(4) Neither house, during the session of Congress, shall, without the consent of the other, adjourn for more than three days, nor to any other place than that in which the two houses shall be sitting.

Section 6. (1) The senators and representatives shall receive a compensation for their services, to be ascertained by law, and paid out of the treasury of the United States. They shall in all cases, except treason, felony and breach of the peace, be privileged from arrest during their attendance at the session of their respective houses, and in going to and returning from the same; and for any speech or debate in either house, they shall not be questioned in any other place.

(2) No senator or representative shall, during the time for which he was elected, be appointed to any civil office under the authority of the United States, which shall have been created, or the emoluments whereof shall have been increased during such time; and no person holding any office under the United States shall be a member of either house during his continuance in office.

Section 7. (1) All bills for raising revenue shall originate in the House of Representatives; but the Senate may propose or concur with amendments as on other bills.

(2) Every bill which shall have passed the House of Representatives and the Senate, shall, before it become a law, be presented to the President of the United States; if he approve he shall sign it, but if not he shall return it, with his objections to that house in which it shall have originated, who shall enter the objections at large on their journal, and proceed to reconsider it. If after such reconsideration two-thirds of that house shall agree to pass the bill, it shall be sent, together with the objections, to the other house, by which it shall likewise be reconsidered, and if approved by two-thirds of that house, it shall become a law. But in all such cases the votes of both houses shall be determined by yeas and nays, and the names of the persons voting for and against the bill shall be entered on the journal of each house respectively. If any bill shall not be returned by the President within ten days (Sundays excepted) after it shall have been presented to him, the same shall be a law, in like manner as if he had signed it, unless the Congress by their

adjournment prevent its return, in which case it shall not be a law.

(3) Every order, resolution, or vote to which the concurrence of the Senate and House of Representatives may be necessary (except on a question of adjournment) shall be presented to the President of the United States; and before the same shall take effect, shall be approved by him, or being disapproved by him, shall be repassed by two-thirds of the Senate and House of Representatives, according to the rules and limitations prescribed in the case of a bill.

Powers Granted to Congress

The Congress shall have power:

Section 8. (1) To lay and collect taxes, duties, imposts and excises, to pay the debts and provide for the common defense and general welfare of the United States; but all duties, imposts and excises shall be uniform throughout the United States;

(2) To borrow money on the credit of the United States;

(3) To regulate commerce with foreign nations, and among the several states, and with the Indian tribes;

(4) To establish an uniform rule of naturalization, and uniform laws on the subject of bankruptcies throughout the United States;

(5) To coin money, regulate the value thereof, and of foreign coin, and fix the standard of weights and measures;

(6) To provide for the punishment of counterfeiting the securities and current coin of the United States;

(7) To establish post offices and post roads;

(8) To promote the progress of science and useful arts, by securing for limited times to authors and inventors the exclusive right to their respective writings and discoveries;

(9) To constitute tribunals inferior to the Supreme Court;

(10) To define and punish piracies and felonies committed on the high seas, and offenses against the law of nations;

(11) To declare war, grant letters of marque and reprisal, and make rules concerning captures on land and water;

(12) To raise and support armies, but no appropriation of money to that use shall be for a longer term than two years;

(13) To provide and maintain a navy;

(14) To make rules for the government and regulation of the land and naval forces;

(15) To provide for calling forth the militia to execute the laws of the Union, suppress insurrections and repel invasions;

(16) To provide for organizing, arming and disciplining the militia, and for governing such part of them as may be employed in the service of the United States, reserving to the states respectively, the appointment of the officers, and the authority of training the militia according to the discipline prescribed by Congress;

(17) To exercise exclusive legislation in all cases whatsoever, over such district (not exceeding ten miles square) as may, by cession of particular states, and the acceptance of Congress, become the seat of the government of the United States, and to exercise like authority over all places purchased by the consent of the legislature of the state in which the same shall be, for the erection of forts, magazines, arsenals, dockyards, and other needful buildings;— And

(18) To make all laws which shall be necessary and proper for carrying into execution the foregoing powers, and all other powers vested by this Constitution in the government of the United States, or in any department or officer thereof.

Powers Forbidden to Congress

Section 9. (1) The migration or importation of such persons as any of the states now existing shall think proper to admit, shall not be prohibited by the Congress prior to the year one thousand eight hundred and eight, but a tax or duty may be imposed on such importation, not exceeding ten dollars for each person.

(2) The privilege of the writ of *habeas corpus* shall not be suspended, unless when in cases of rebellion or invasion the public safety may require it.

(3) No bill of attainder or *ex post facto* law shall be passed.

(4) No capitation, [or other direct,] tax shall be laid, unless in proportion to the census or enumeration herein before directed to be taken.

(5) No tax or duty shall be laid on articles exported from any state.

(6) No preference shall be given by any regulation of commerce or revenue to the ports of one state over those of another: nor shall vessels bound to, or from, one state, be obliged to enter, clear, or pay duties in another.

(7) No money shall be drawn from the treasury, but in consequence of appropriations made by law; and a regular statement and account of the receipts and expenditures of all public money shall be published from time to time.

(8) No title of nobility shall be granted by the United States: And no person holding any office or profit or trust under them, shall, without the consent of the Congress, accept of any present, emolument, office, or title, of any kind whatsoever, from any king, prince, or foreign state.

Powers Forbidden to the States

Section 10. (1) No state shall enter into any treaty, alliance, or confederation; grant letters of marque and reprisal; coin money; emit bills of credit; make any thing but gold and silver coin a tender in payment of debts; pass any bill of attainder, *ex post facto* law, or law impairing the obligation of contracts, or grant any title of nobility.

(2) No state shall, without the consent of the Congress, lay any imposts or duties on imports or exports, except what may be absolutely necessary for executing its inspection laws: and the net produce of all duties and imposts, laid by any state on imports or exports, shall be for the use of the treasury of the United States, and all such laws shall be subject to the revision and control of the Congress.

(3) No state shall, without the consent of Congress, lay any duty of tonnage, keep troops, or ships of war in time of peace, enter into any agreement or compact with another state, or with a foreign power, or engage in war, unless actually invaded, or in such imminent danger as will not admit of delay.

Article II
The Executive Branch

Section 1. (1) The executive power shall be vested in a President of the United States of America. He shall hold his office during the term of four years, and, together with the Vice President, chosen for the same term, be elected as follows:

(2) Each state shall appoint, in such manner as the legislature thereof may direct, a number of electors, equal to the whole number of senators and representatives to which the state may be entitled in the Congress: but no senator or representative, or person holding an office of trust or profit under the United States, shall be appointed an elector.

(3) [The electors shall meet in their respective states, and vote by ballot for two persons, of whom one at least shall not be an inhabitant of the same state with themselves. And they shall make a list of all the persons voted for, and of the number of votes for each; which list they shall sign and certify, and transmit sealed to the seat of government of the United States, directed to the president of the Senate. The president of the Senate shall, in the presence of the Senate and House of Representatives, open all the certificates, and the votes shall then be counted. The person having the greatest number of votes shall be the President, if such number be a majority of the whole number of electors appointed; and if there be more than one who have such majority, and have an equal number of votes, then the House of Representatives shall immediately choose by ballot one of them for President; and if no person have a majority, then from the five highest on the list the said House shall in like manner choose the President. But in choosing the President, the votes shall be taken by states, the representation from each state having one vote; a quorum for this purpose shall consist of a member or members from two-thirds of the states, and a majority of all the states shall be necessary to a choice. In every case, after the choice of the President, the person having the greatest number of votes of the electors shall be the Vice President. But if there should remain two or more who have equal votes, the Senate shall choose from them by ballot the Vice President.]

(4) The Congress may determine the time of choosing the electors, and the day on which they shall give their votes; which day shall be the same throughout the United States.

(5) No person except a natural-born citizen, or a citizen of the United States, at the time of the adoption of this Constitution, shall be eligible to the office of President; neither shall any person be eligible to that office who shall not have attained to the age of thirty-five years, and been fourteen years a resident within the United States.

(6) In case of the removal of the President from office, or of his death, resignation, or inability to discharge the powers and duties of the said office, the same shall devolve on the Vice President, and the Congress may by law provide for the case of removal, death, resignation or inability, both of the President and Vice President, declaring what officer shall then act as President, and such officer shall act accordingly, until the disability be removed, or a President shall be elected.

(7) The President shall, at stated times, receive for his services, a compensation, which shall neither be increased nor diminished during the period for which he shall have been elected, and he shall not receive within that period any other emolument from the United States, or any of them.

(8) Before he enter on the execution of his office, he shall take the following oath or affirmation: "I do solemnly swear (or affirm) that I will faithfully execute the office of the President of the United States, and will to the best of my ability, preserve, protect and defend the Constitution of the United States."

Section 2. (1) The President shall be commander-in-chief of the Army and Navy of the United States, and of the militia of the several states, when called into the actual service of the United States; he may require the opinion, in writing, of the principal officer in each of the executive departments, upon any subject relating to the duties of their respective offices, and he shall have power to grant reprieves and pardons for offenses against the United States, except in cases of impeachment.

(2) He shall have power, by and with the advice and consent of the Senate, to make treaties, provided two-thirds of the senators present concur; and he shall nominate, and by and with the advice and consent of the Senate, shall appoint ambassadors, other public ministers and consuls, judges of the Supreme Court, and all other officers of the United States, whose appointments are not herein otherwise provided for, and which shall be established by law: but the Congress may by law vest the appointment of such inferior officers, as they think proper, in the President alone, in the courts of law, or in the heads of departments.

(3) The President shall have the power to fill up all vacancies that may happen during the recess of the Senate, by granting commissions which shall expire at the end of their next session.

Section 3. He shall from time to time give to the Congress information of the state of the Union, and recommend to their consideration such measures as he shall judge necessary and expedient; he may, on extraordinary occasions, convene both houses, or either of them, and in case of disagreement between them, with respect to the time of adjournment, he may adjourn them to such time as he shall think proper; he shall receive ambassadors and other public ministers; he shall take care that the laws be faithfully executed, and shall commission all the officers of the United States.

Section 4. The President, Vice President and all civil officers of the United States, shall be removed from office on impeachment for, and conviction of, treason, bribery, or other high crimes and misdemeanors.

ARTICLE III
The Judicial Branch

Section 1. The judicial power of the United States, shall be vested in one Supreme Court, and in such inferior courts as the Congress may from time to time ordain and establish. The judges, both of the Supreme and inferior courts, shall hold their offices during good behaviour, and shall, at stated times, receive for their services, a compensation, which shall not be diminished during their continuance in office.

Section 2. (1) The judicial power shall extend to all cases, in law and equity, arising under this Constitution, the laws of the United States, and treaties made, or which shall be made, under their authority; —to all cases affecting ambassadors, other public ministers and consuls;—to all cases of admiralty and maritime jurisdiction;—to controversies to which the United States shall be a party;—to controversies between two or more states, [between a state and citizens of another state;], between citizens of different states;—between citizens of the same state claiming lands under grants of different states, and between a state, or the citizens thereof, and foreign states, [citizens or subjects].

(2) In all cases affecting ambassadors, other public ministers and consuls, and those in which a state shall be party, the Supreme Court shall have original jurisdiction. In all the other cases before mentioned, the Supreme Court shall have appellate jurisdiction, both as to law and fact, with such exceptions, and under such regulations as the Congress shall make.

(3) The trial of all crimes, except in cases of impeachment, shall be by jury; and such trial shall be held in the state where the said crimes shall have been committed; but when not committed within any state, the trial shall be at such place or places as the Congress may by law have directed.

Section 3. (1) Treason against the United States, shall consist only in levying war against them, or in adhering to their enemies, giving them aid and comfort. No person shall be convicted of treason unless on the testimony of two witnesses to the same overt act, or on confession in open court.

(2) The Congress shall have power to declare the punishment of treason, but no attainder of treason shall work corruption of blood, or forfeiture, except during the life of the person attainted.

ARTICLE IV
Relation of the States to Each Other

Section 1. Full faith and credit shall be given in each state to the public acts, records, and judicial proceedings of every other state. And the Congress may by general laws prescribe the manner in which such acts, records and proceedings shall be proved, and the effect thereof.

Section 2. (1) The citizens of each state shall be entitled to all privileges and immunities of citizens in the several states.

(2) A person charged in any state with treason, felony, or other crime, who shall flee justice, and be found in another state, shall on demand of the executive authority of the state from which he fled, be delivered up, to be removed to the state having jurisdiction of the crime.

(3) [No person held to service or labor in one state, under the laws thereof, escaping into another, shall, in consequence of any law or regulation therein, be discharged from such service or labor, but shall be delivered up on claim of the party to whom such service or labor may be due.]

Federal-State Relations

Section 3. (1) New states may be admitted by the Congress into this Union; but no new state shall be formed or erected within the jurisdiction of any other state, nor any state be formed by the junction of two or more states, without the consent of the legislatures of the states concerned as well as of the Congress.

(2) The Congress shall have power to dispose of and make all needful rules and regulations respecting the territory or other property belonging to the United States; and nothing in this Constitution shall be so construed as to prejudice any claims of the United States, or of any particular state.

Section 4. The United States shall guarantee to every state in this Union a republican form of government, and shall protect each of them against invasion; and on application of the legislature, or of the executive (when the legislature cannot be convened), against domestic violence.

ARTICLE V
Amending the Constitution

The Congress, whenever two-thirds of both houses shall deem it necessary, shall propose amendments to this Constitution, or, on the application of the legislatures of two-thirds of the several states, shall call a convention for proposing amendments, which, in either case, shall be valid to all intents and purposes, as part of this Constitution, when ratified by the legislatures of three-fourths of the several states, or by conventions in three-fourths thereof, as the one or the other mode of ratification may be proposed by the Congress; provided [that no amendment which may be made prior to the year one thousand eight hundred and eight, shall in any manner affect the first and fourth clauses in the ninth section of the first article; and] that no state, without its consent, shall be deprived of its equal suffrage in the Senate.

ARTICLE VI
National Debts

(1) All debts contracted and engagements entered into, before the adoption of this Constitution, shall be as

valid against the United States under this Constitution, as under the Confederation.

Supremacy of the National Government

(2) This Constitution, and the laws of the United States which shall be made in pursuance thereof; and all treaties made, or which shall be made, under the authority of the United States shall be the supreme law of the land; and the judges in every state shall be bound thereby, any thing in the constitution or laws of any state to the contrary notwithstanding.

(3) The senators and representatives before mentioned, and the members of the several state legislatures, and all executive and judicial officers, both of the United States and of the several states, shall be bound by oath or affirmation, to support this Constitution; but no religious test shall ever be required as a qualification to any office or public trust under the United States.

ARTICLE VII
Ratifying the Constitution

The ratification of the conventions of nine states, shall be sufficient for the establishment of this Constitution between the states so ratifying the same.

Done in convention by the unanimous consent of the states present the seventeenth day of September in the year of our Lord one thousand seven hundred and eighty-seven and of the independence of the United States of America the twelfth. In witness whereof we have hereunto subscribed our names.

Amendments to the Constitution

The first ten amendments, known as the Bill of Rights, were proposed on September 25, 1789. They were ratified, or accepted, on December 15, 1791. They were adopted because some states refused to approve the Constitution unless a Bill of Rights, protecting individuals from various unjust acts of government, was added.

Amendment 1

Freedom of religion, speech, and the press;
rights of assembly and petition

Amendment 2

Right to bear arms

Amendment 3

Housing of soldiers

Amendment 4

Search and arrest warrants

Amendment 5

Rights in criminal cases

Amendment 6

Rights to a fair trial

Amendment 7

Rights in civil cases

Amendment 8

Bails, fines, and punishments

Amendment 9

Rights retained by the people

Amendment 10

Powers retained by the states and the people

Amendment 11

Lawsuits against states

Amendment 12

Election of the President and Vice President

Amendment 13

Abolition of slavery

Amendment 14

Civil rights

Amendment 15
African-American suffrage

Amendment 16
Income taxes

Amendment 17
Direct election of senators

Amendment 18
Prohibition of liquor

Amendment 19
Women's suffrage

Amendment 20
Terms of the President and Congress

Amendment 21
Repeal of prohibition

Amendment 22
Presidential term limits

Amendment 23
Suffrage in the District of Columbia

Amendment 24
Poll taxes

Amendment 25
Presidential disability and succession

Amendment 26
Suffrage for eighteen-year-olds

Amendment 27
Congressional salaries

Chapter Notes

Chapter 1

1. Elizabeth Cady Stanton, *Eighty Years & More: Reminiscences 1815–1897* (New York: Schocken Books, 1971), p. 148.

2. Ibid.

3. Ibid.

4. Eleanor Flexner, *Century of Struggle: The Woman's Rights Movement in the United States* (Cambridge, Mass.: The Belknap Press of Harvard University Press, 1975), p. 74.

5. The Commission on the Bicentennial of the United States Constitution, *1791–1991: The Bill of Rights and Beyond* (Washington, D.C.: U.S. Congress, 1991), p. 72.

6. Flexner, p. 74.

7. Ibid., p. 43.

8. Carol Hymowitz and Michaele Weissman, *A History of Women in America* (New York: Bantam Books, 1978), p. 97.

9. Mari Jo and Paul Buhle, eds., *The Concise History of Women Suffrage* (Urbana, Ill.: University of Illinois Press, 1978), p. 97.

10. Stanton, p. 150.

11. Ibid., p. 149.

12. *Women's Rights*, National Park Service, Washington, D.C.: U.S. Department of the Interior, 1994.

Chapter 2

1. Marjorie Spruil Wheeler, ed., *One Woman, One Vote* (Troutdale, Oreg.: NewSage Press and Educational Film Company, 1995), p. 24

2. Ibid., p. 25.

3. William Dudley, ed., *The Creation of the Constitution: Opposing Viewpoints* (San Diego, Calif.: Greenhaven Press, Inc., 1995), p. 27.

4. Ibid., p. 48.

5. J. W. Peltason, *Corwin & Peltason's Understanding the Constitution* (San Diego, Calif.: Harcourt Brace Jovanovich, Publishers, 1991), p. 15.

6. Linda Carlson Johnson, *Our Constitution* (Brookfield, Conn.: The Millbrook Press, 1992), pp. 33–34.

7. Dudley, p. 273.

8. Wheeler, p. 21.

9. Doris Faber and Harold Faber, *We the People: The Story of the United States Constitution Since 1787* (New York: Charles Scribner's Sons, 1987), pp. 150–151.

10. United States Constitution, Article I, section 2.

Chapter 3

1. Sally Roesch Wagner, *The Declaration of Rights of Women: 1876* (Aberdeen, S.D.: North Plains Press, 1975), p. 15.

2. Madeleine Meyers, *Forward into Light: The Struggle for Woman's Suffrage* (Lowell, Mass.: Discovery Enterprises, Ltd., 1994), p. 8.

3. Ibid., pp. 8–9.

4. Edith Mayo, Introduction to *Jailed for Freedom: American Women Win the Vote*, by Doris Stevens, (Troutdale, Oreg.: NewSage Press, 1995), p. 13.

5. Carol Hymowitz and Michaele Weissman, *A History of Women in America* (New York: Bantam Books, 1978), p. 185.

6. Eleanor Flexner, *Century of Struggle: The Woman's Rights Movements in the United States* (Cambridge, Mass.: The Belknap Press of Harvard University Press, 1975), p. 178.

7. Ibid., p. 181.

8. Susan B. Anthony, in "Arguments of the Woman-Suffrage Delegates Before the Committee on the Judiciary of the United States Senate," January 23, 1880, 47th Congress, 1st Session, p. 16.

9. Flexner, p. 168.

10. Wagner, p. 25.

11. Ibid., p. 26.

12. Ibid., p. 34.

13. Julia Smith Parker, in "Arguments of the Woman-Suffrage Delegates Before the Committee on the Judiciary of the United States Senate," January 23, 1880, 47th Congress, 1st Session, p. 4.

14. Nancy C. Allen, in "Arguments of the Woman-Suffrage Delegates Before the Committee on the Judiciary of the United States Senate," January 23, 1880, 47th Congress, 1st Session, p. 10.

15. Hymowitz and Weissman, p. 271.

16. Flexner, p. 271.

17. Marjorie Spruil Wheeler, ed., *One Woman, One Vote* (Troutdale, Oreg.: NewSage Press, 1995), p. 159.

18. Ibid.

19. Flexner, p. 278.

20. Ibid., p. 258.

21. Ibid., p. 273 .

22. Inez Haynes Irwin, *The Story of Alice Paul and The National Women's Party* (Fairfax, Va.: Delinger's Publishers, Ltd., 1977), p. 31.

23. Ibid., p. 34.

24. Flexner, p. 284.

25. Ibid.

26. Doris Faber and Harold Faber, *We the People: The Story of the United States Constitution Since 1787* (New York: Charles Scribner's Sons, 1987), p. 162.

27. Mari Jo and Paul Bunke, eds., *The Concise History, of Women's Suffrage* (Urbana, Ill.: University of Illinois Press, 1978), p. 39.

28. Irwin, p. 129.

29. Ibid.

30. Ibid., p. 203.

31. Sherna Gluck, ed., *From Parlor to Prison: Five American Suffragists Talk About Their Lives* (New York: Vintage Books, 1976), p. 21.

32. Mari Jo and Paul Buhle, p. 220.

33. Gluck, pp. 243–244.

34. Ibid., p. 247.

35. Ibid., p.214.

Chapter 4

1. Sherna Gluck, *From Parlor to Prison: Five American Suffragists Talk About Their Lives* (New York: Vintage Books, 1976), p. 190.

2.. Ibid., p. 203.

3. Ibid., p. 204.

4. Ibid., p. 205.

5. Barbara Stuhler, *Gentle Warriors: Clara Ueland and the Minnesota Struggle for Woman Suffrage* (St. Paul, Minn.: Minnesota Historical Society Press, 1995), p. 83.

6. Ibid., pp. 99–100.

7. Ibid., p. 100.

8. Ibid., p. 175.

9. Ibid., p. 214.

Chapter 5

1. Eleanor Flexner, *Century of Struggle: The Woman's Rights Movement in the United States* (Cambridge, Mass.: Harvard University Press, 1975), p. 288.

2. Woodrow Wilson Address, NAWSA Convention, Atlantic City, NJ, September 4–10, 1916; Mari Jo and Paul Buhle, eds., *The Concise History of Women Suffrage*, (Urbana, Ill: University of Illinois Press, 1978), p. 434.

3. Mary Gray Peck, *Carrie Chapman Catt: A Biography* (New York: The H.W. Wilson Company, 1944), pp. 260–261.

4. Ibid., p. 263.

5. Ibid., pp. 267–268.

6. Flexner, p. 294.

7. Inez Haynes Irwin, *The Story of Alice Paul and the National Women's Party* (Fairfax, Va.: Denlinger's Publisher's, LTD., 1977), p. 292.

8. Congressional Record, *"Women Suffrage," Report No. 219, House of Representatives,* 65th Congress, Second Session, December 15, 1917.

9. Flexner, p. 301.

10. J. Stanley Lemons, *The Woman Citizen: Social Feminism in the 1920s* (Charlottesville, Va.: University Press of Virignia, 1973), p. 5.

11. 65th Cong., H.R. 219, (1917).

12. 65th Cong., H.R. 234, (1918).

13. Ibid.

14. Ibid.

15. Ibid.

16. Peck, p. 288.

17. Ibid., p. 289.

18. "Votes for Women!! Celebrates 75 Years," *Her Own Words*, Spring 1995, Thorson Enterprises, Women's History & Literature Media web page.

19. Peck, p. 319.

20. Ibid., pp. 330–331.

21. Marjorie Spruill Wheeler, ed., *Votes for Women!* (Knoxville, Tenn.: The University of Tennessee Press, 1995), pp. 63–64.

22. Flexner, p. 336.

23. Peck, p. 336.

24. Ibid., p. 337.

25. Ibid.

26. Barbara Stuhler, *Gentle Warriors: Clara Ueland and the Minnesota Struggle for Woman Suffrage* (St. Paul, Minn.: Minnesota Historical Society Press, 1995), p. 178.

27. Bill Severn, *Free But Not Equal: How Women Won the Right to Vote* (New York: Julian Messner, 1967), p. 179.

Chapter 6

1. The Commission on the Bicentennial of the United States Constitution, *1791–1991: The Bill of Rights and Beyond* (Washington, D.C.: U.S. Congress, 1991), p. 74.

2. J. Stanley Lemons, *The Woman Citizen: Social Feminism in the 1920s* (Charlottesville, Va.: University Press of Virginia, 1973), p. 63.

3. Doris Stevens, *Jailed for Freedom: American Women Win the Vote* (Troutdale, Oreg.: NewSage Press, 1995), p. 201.

4. Mary Gray Peck, *Carrie Chapman Catt: A Biography* (New York: The H.W. Wilson Company, 1944), p. 306.

5. Barbara Stuhler, *Gentle Warriors: Clara Ueland and the Minnesota Struggle for Woman Suffrage* (St. Paul, Minn.: Minnesota Historical Society Press, 1995), p. 190.

6. Ibid., pp. 203–204.

7. Doris Faber and Harold Faber, *We the People: The Story of the United States Constitution Since 1787* (New York: Charles Scribner's Sons, 1987), p. 164.

8. Connie Cass, "GOP recalls suffrage days of long ago to lure women," *San Jose Mercury News*, August 26, 1995, at http://newslibrary.infini.net/sj/

9. Lemons, p. 51.

10. Ibid.

11. Ibid., p. 406.

12. Stuhler, p. 205.

13. Jean E. Friedman, William G. Shade, and Mary Jane Capozzoli, *Our American Sisters: Women in American Life and Thought* (Lexington, Mass.: D.C. Health and Company, 1987), p. 416.

14. Lemons, pp. 173, 174.

15. Friedman, p. 418.

16. Ibid.

17. Lois Scharf and Joan M. Jensen, *Decades of Discontent: The Women's Movement, 1920–1940* (Boston, Mass.: Northeastern University Press, 1983), p. 6.

18. Sherna Gluck, *From Parlor to Prison: Five American Suffragists Talk About Their Lives* (New York: Vintage Books, 1976), p. 214.

19. Stuhler, p. 207.

20. Gluck, p. 215.

21. Lemons, p. 110.

22. Carole Lynn Corbin, *The Right to Vote: Issues in American History* (New York: Franklin Watts, 1985), p. 82.

Chapter 7

1. Doris Stevens, *Jailed for Freedom: American Women Win the Vote* (Troutdale, Oreg.: NewSage Press, 1995), p. 201.

2. Ibid., p. 202.

3. Ibid.

4. Mark Curnutte, "Women's Struggle for vote too little respected," *San Jose Mercury News*, August 26, 1995, at http://newslibrary.infini.net/sj/

5. Lois Romano, "When Women Got the Vote," *Good Housekeeping*, March 1995, p. 90.

6. Ibid., p. 91.

7. Ibid., p. 92.

8. Tom Raum, "After aiding Clinton's re-election, women's groups seek their reward," *Saint Paul Pioneer Press*, December 1, 1996, p. 26A.

9. Ibid.

10. Marilyn Lewis, "Seventy-Five Years and no Female President," *San Jose Mercury News*, August 26, 1995, at http://http://newslibrary.infini.net/sj/

11. Curnutte.

Glossary

amendment—New provisions to the Constitution, or changes to a particular portion of the Constitution.

American Woman Suffrage Association (AWSA)—Founded by Lucy Stone, Julia Ward Howe, and Henry Ward Beecher, the AWSA worked for gradual adoption of women's suffrage on a state-by-state basis.

Articles of Confederation—In 1781 this document created a weak central government for all American states, but one with limited power.

bill—A suggested law or proposal that could become law if passed by the House of Representatives and the Senate and signed by the President.

Bill of Rights—The first ten amendments to the United States Constitution. They protect the rights of individuals. The Bill of Rights gives Americans many freedoms and protections such as freedom of religion, speech, and the press.

Centennial Exposition—America's one hundredth birthday celebration held in Philadelphia during the summer of 1876.

Civil War—The war between the Union (the North) and the Confederacy (the South) from 1861 to 1865.

Congress—Made up of elected representatives in the House and Senate. It has the power to make the country's laws and raise money for government use.

Declaration of Independence—Passed in 1776, this document guaranteed freedom for all Americans.

Declaration of Sentiments—A set of resolutions or specific requests passed by the three hundred people attending the Seneca Falls Convention in New York in 1848.

Equal Right Amendment (ERA)—A propopsal to ensure equal pay for men and women for the same jobs, the National Woman's Party began to lobby for another amendment right after the Nineteenth Amendment was passed. The ERA was passed by Congress in 1972, however it was not ratified by the three-quarters of the states as required, so the proposal died.

House of Representatives—One of the two legislative branches of the United States Congress that makes laws.

National American Woman Suffrage Association (NAWSA)—Formed in 1890 with the merging of the National Woman's Suffrage Association and the American Woman Suffrage Association. The group fought for suffrage on both the federal level, by supporting an amendment, and on a state-by-state basis.

National League of Women Voters (NLWV)— Formed by Carrie Chapman Catt as part of the NAWSA in 1919. It became independent a year later. Headquartered in New York City, this organization helps women learn about politics and voting.

National Woman Suffrage Association (NWSA)—A national, pro-suffrage organization that helped fight for the passage of the Nineteenth Amendment. It was created by Elizabeth Cady Stanton and Susan B. Anthony.

National Women's Party (NWP)—Pro-suffrage, national organization formed by Alice Paul. It directed ongoing campaigns against the political party in power, then directly on the president in power, Woodrow Wilson.

Nineteenth Amendment—Ratified on August 18, 1920, this amendment to the United States Constitution gave women the right to vote in all elections.

nullify—To repeal or remove.

ratify—To accept.

resolution—A specific request.

Senate—One of the two legislative branches of the United States Congress that makes laws.

Seneca Falls Convention—The first women's rights convention in the United States, held in Seneca Falls, New York, on July 19–20, 1848.

suffrage—Women's right to vote.

Supreme Court—The highest court in the United States. It interprets laws and the United States Constitution. The Supreme Court has the power to decide whether a law is constitutional.

United States Constitution—The highest law of America. This document, which went into effect in 1787, covers the basic laws and principles on which America is governed.

Woman's Political Union (WPU)—Harriet Stanton Blatch formed this pro-suffrage, national organization in January 1907.

Further Reading

Buhle, Mari Jo and Paul, eds. *The Concise History of Woman Suffrage*. Urbana, Ill: University of Illinois Press, 1978.

The Commission on the Bicentennial of the United States Constitution, *1791–1991: The Bill of Rights and Beyond*. Washington, D.C.: U.S. Congress, 1991.

Cullen-DuPont, Kathryn. *Elizabeth Cady Stanton and Women's Liberty*. New York: Facts on File, 1992.

Dudley, William, ed. *The Creation of the Constitution: Opposing Viewpoints*. San Diego, Calif.: Greenhaven Press, Inc., 1995.

Faber, Doris and Harold Faber. *We the People: The Story of the United States Constitution Since 1787*. New York: Charles Scribner's Sons, 1987.

Flexner, Eleanor. *Century of Struggle: The Woman's Rights Movement in the United States*. Cambridge, Mass.: The Belknap Press of Harvard University Press, 1975.

Fowler, Robert Booth. *Carrie Catt: Feminist Politician*. Boston: Northeastern University Press, 1986.

Fritz, Jean. *You Want Women to Vote, Lizzie Stanton?* New York: Putnam Publishing Group, 1995.

Gluck, Sherna., ed. *From Parlor to Prison: Five American Suffragists Talk About Their Lives*. New York: Vintage Books, 1976.

Irwin, Inez Hayes. *The Story of Alice Paul and The National Women's Party*. Fairfax, Va.: Delinger's Publishers, Ltd., 1977.

Johnson, Linda Carlson. *Our Constitution*. Brookfield, Conn.: The Millbrook Press, 1992.

Noble, Iris. *Susan B. Anthony*. New York: Julian. Messner Publishers, 1975.

Peck, Mary Gray. *Carrie Chapman Catt: A Biography.* New York: The H.W. Wilson Company, 1944.

Peltason, J.W. *Corwin & Peltason's Understanding the Constitution.* San Diego, Calif.: Harcourt Brace Jovanovich, Publishers, 1991.

Severn, Bill. *Free But Not Equal: How Women Won the Right to Vote.* New York: Julian Messner Publishers, 1967.

Smith, Betsy Covington. *Women Win the Vote.* Englewood Cliffs, N.J.: Silver Burdett Press, 1989.

Stanton, Elizabeth Cady. *Eighty Years & More: Reminiscences 1815–1897.* New York: Schocken Books, 1971.

Stevens, Doris. *Jailed for Freedom: American Women Win the Vote.* Troutdale, Oeg.: NewSage Press, 1995.

Stuhler, Barbara. *Gentle Warriors: Clara Ueland and the Minnesota Struggle for Woman Suffrage.* St. Paul, Minn.: Minnesota Historical Society Press, 1995.

Van Voris, Jacqueline. *Carrie Chapman Catt: A Public Life.* New York: Feminist Press at the City University of New York, 1987.

Wheeler, Marjorie Spruil. ed. *One Woman, One Vote.* Troutdale, Oreg.: NewSage Press and Educational Film Company, 1995.

Index

League of Women Voters (LWV), 80, 83, 84–85, 87, 91

M

McClintock, Mary Ann, 9
Madison, James, 16, 17, 18–19, 20
Marshall, Vice President, 71
Minnesota League of Women's Voters, 56, 58
Minnesota Woman Suffrage Association (MWSA), 51, 56, 58
Moseley-Braun, Senator Carol, 89
Mott, Lucretia, 9, 10–12, 92
Mott Amendment, *see* Equal Rights Amendment

N

National American Woman Suffrage Association (NAWSA), 36–38, 41, 43–45, 48–49, 56, 60, 61–62, 63, 69, 71, 72, 80, 83, 84
National League of Women's Voters (NLWV), *See also* League of Women's Voters
National Organzation for Women (NOW), 87
National Woman Suffrage Association (NWSA), 29, 32–34, 35
National Woman's Party (NWP), 45–48, 62, 77, 80, 84, 92
Nineteenth Amendment, *See also* Amendment, Nineteenth

O

O'Connor, Sandra Day, 88–89
Olesen, Anna Dickie, 83

P

Panhurst, Emmeline, 39
Park, Maud Wood, 77
Parker, Julia Smith, 35
Paul, Alice, 38, 40–43, 45–46, 47, 51, 60, 62–63, 70, 71, 77, 80
Proclamation of the Women's Suffrage Amendment, 77

R

Rankin, Jeanette, 61
Raker, Judge, 67–69

Roberts, Albert H., 73
Rush, Benjamin, 16–17

S

Schroeder, Pat, 88
Seiler, Laura Ellsworth, 48, 51–55, 85, 86
Seneca Falls Convention, 7, 10, 12–13, 15, 25, 27, 82, 91
Shaw, Dr. Anna, 36, 37, 41, 43, 44
Shays, Daniel, 17
Shays' Rebellion, 17
Sheppard-Towner Act, 84
Stanton, Elizabeth Cady, 9, 10, 12, 13, 29, 33, 37, 51, 92
Stewart, Potter, 89
Stone, Lucy, 29, 51
Stowe, Harriet Beecher, 36
Suffrage Amendment, *see* Amendments, Nineteenth

T

Thatcher, Margaret, 90
Turner, Banks, 75

U

Ueland, Clara, 51, 55–56, 58
United States Constitution, *See also* Constitution
Upton, Harriet Taylor, 77

W

Washington, George, 16, 17–18
Willard, Frances, 35–36
Wilson, President Woodrow, 41, 42–43, 44, 45–48, 60–62, 67, 69–71, 73
women
    education, 38
    employment, 13, 27, 38, 59, 79, 85
    lack of rights, 24–25, 27–28, 33, 79
    rights conventions, 7, 9–10, 13, 25, 27
Women's Christian Temperance Union (WCTU), 35–36
Women's Joint Congressional Committee (WJCC), 84
Woman's Political Union (WPU), 39–40, 52–55